Contents

References in these Notes are to the
Penguin edition of *The Crucible*, but as reference
is made to individual acts, the Notes may be
used with any edition of the play.

Preface

The intention throughout this study aid is to stimulate and guide, to encourage your involvement in the book, and to develop informed responses and a sure understanding of the main details.

Brodie's Notes provide a clear outline of the play or novel's plot, followed by act, scene, or chapter summaries and/or commentaries. These are designed to emphasize the most important literary and factual details. Poems, stories or non-fiction texts combine brief summary with critical commentary on individual aspects or common features of the genre being examined. Textual notes define what is difficult or obscure and emphasize literary qualities. Revision questions are set at appropriate points to test your ability to appreciate the prescribed book and to write accurately and relevantly about it.

In addition, each of these Notes includes a critical appreciation of the author's art. This covers such major elements as characterization, style, structure, setting and themes. Poems are examined technically – rhyme, rhythm, for instance. In fact, any important aspect of the prescribed work will be evaluated. The aim is to send you back to the text you are studying.

Each study aid concludes with a series of general questions which require a detailed knowledge of the book: some of these questions may invite comparison with other books, some will be suitable for coursework exercises, and some could be adapted to work you are doing on another book or books. Each study aid has been adapted to meet the needs of the current examination requirements. They provide a basic, individual and imaginative response to the work being studied, and it is hoped that they will stimulate you to acquire disciplined reading habits and critical fluency.

Graham Handley 1990

To the student

1 There are two readily available and convenient texts of *The Crucible* in The Penguin Plays (1968) and the school edition edited by E. R. Wood (Heinemann, 1967), which also has a brief introduction. In these Notes, where page references are given, the *first* is to the Penguin edition. For convenience, page references have also been inserted for the Notes, which tend to be only thinly scattered among the four Acts.

2 These Notes are not designed to replace a very close reading and re-reading of the text itself: they must be considered complementary to such careful reading and no substitute for it. The play is often performed by local repertory companies, and obviously should be seen as a live performance if at all possible.

3 There are many useful and interesting books available on Arthur Miller: in most instances, too much detail should be avoided, and the index used for particular references.
(a) Miller's own Introduction to his *Collected Plays* (Cresset, 1958) is not simple, but contains many valuable insights.
(b) *Arthur Miller: Portrait of a Playwright*, by Benjamin Nelson (Peter Owen, 1970): detailed and sympathetic, with a careful analysis of each major play.
(c) *Arthur Miller*, by Ronald Hayman (Heinemann, 1970): useful and easily read, but slight.
(d) *Arthur Miller*, by Dennis Welland (Oliver & Boyd, 1961): fairly detailed, with an excellent bibliography.
(e) *Time Bends*, by Arthur Miller (Methuen, 1987).

4 The student is not recommended to spend too much time on the topics of Puritanism and witchcraft, on both of which there is considerable literature. Any general history book will provide the religious background: the book which particularly interested Arthur Miller on witchcraft was *The Devil in Massachusetts*, by M. L. Starkey (Doubleday, New York). In the magazine *History Makers* issue No. 3, of 1969, there is a good article on the Salem Trials. Many reference libraries hold bound copies of this journal. In general, the basic material can be gleaned from any good encyclopedia.

The author and his work

Arthur Miller was born (October 17, 1915) in New York to a middle-class non-orthodox Jewish family: his mother had been a teacher, and his father was, at that time, a successful and well-to-do manufacturer of ladies' coats. The boy was fonder of and better at games than work, and did not distinguish himself at his first or subsequent schools when the family moved to Brooklyn, near Coney Island. He played games vigorously, fished and surfed, did an early-morning delivery-round (starting at 5 o'clock!) despite a knee-injury sustained at one of the games he enjoyed: but he made little headway with more formal, academic work. In 1929 a severe economic depression hit the United States: the Millers, among millions of others, lost most of their money and security; when Arthur Miller graduated from High School he had neither the financial nor the academic background necessary for entry into University. He therefore reluctantly tried his hand at a series of jobs: in the garment industry, as a truck driver, a waiter, a crooner on a local radio-station, a tanker-crewman, and as a shipping clerk at $15 a week. In all these diverse occupations the young man noted and reflected on the enormous variety of people, the acute tensions of materialist society, and anti-semitism: these were themes later to be developed in his writing.

In 1934, having saved as much as he could from his meagre earnings, he applied as a mature entrant into Michigan University, and was accepted. He had much to learn, and much academic background material to master; but he loved the University and its atmosphere, with its diverse population of undergraduates and staff, finding his niche eventually in the English Department under sympathetic teachers. There he won two awards in an annual competition for original playwriting, each of $250; but when he graduated in 1938 he was unemployed. For a short spell he worked for an ill-fated Federal Theatre project, and when this collapsed he once more took up a number of manual jobs: again as truck driver and a steamfitter. In 1940 he married a college friend, Mary Slattery, and, rejected as unfit for military service because of his old knee-injury, he divided his time between manual war-work at the shipyards and free-lance radio script-writing. His wife helped by secretarial employment. At this time Miller wrote many radio-scripts and then plays: some were patriotic as the times demanded, some were purely experimental – but he was much more interested in the live theatre, and in 1944 came his first Broadway play *The Man Who Had All the Luck*. The title was ironic: the play was a dismal failure, closing after four performances at a loss for its backers of $55,000. It was an inauspicious start.

More successfully, he wrote a documentary narrative *Situation Normal*, based on widely and sensitively collected material he was asked to gather for a film about the American Army: reviewers commented favourably on his close and keen observation; and in 1945 he wrote *Focus*, a novel concerned with anti-semitism with the themes of personal integrity and social responsibility explored keenly and searchingly. Miller was strongly and increasingly engaged in working out the curious nature of human relationships, especially under social, economic, and religious strains in particular and delicate situations; and this, after much painstaking exploration and constant re-drafting, emerged eventually into his first positive professional dramatic success of *All My Sons* (1947), awarded the New York Drama Critics' Circle Award. It ran for 328 performances and was praised for its 'dramatic sense, human sense, and moral sense': a new young playwright, a new important talent, had made a successful mark. The play ran too into foreign productions (for example in London, Paris and Stockholm), and was filmed in 1948 with Edward G. Robinson in the central role of the small factory owner who, in order to save a wartime government contract, permits the sale of damaged aeroplane engines to the Air Force with terrible consequent losses of human life: he eventually commits suicide. This success was followed by a greater, possibly the best American play of its kind ever written, *Death of a Salesman* (1949). This ran for 742 performances, was highly praised, won many further awards, and the playwright had reinforced his growing reputation by an extraordinarily complex yet realistic and powerful play, which is, as has been said, 'probably the only successful twentieth-century tragedy with an unheroic hero'. Willy Loman is the elderly exhausted travelling salesman whose life and family have become hollow,

deteriorated, falsified by the whole propaganda of sales pro-
motion and false advertisement: most of the play is a piercing
revelation of what goes on in his mind, and he, too is driven to
his death. With sensitive use of flash-back techniques, of powerful evocative language in a range of rhythms, and persistent
agonizing analysis of human integrity, the play remains a haunting theatrical experience.

After an unsuccessful adaptation of Ibsen's *An Enemy of the
People, The Crucible* followed in 1953. Its (and Miller's) relationship to what is called McCarthyism is considered in a later
separate section. It ran well after considerable critical acclaim,
and won several awards for distinguished drama, and was later
televised, with George C. Scott as Proctor, in a remarkably fine
and memorable portrayal. In 1956, amid all the turmoil of the
McCarthy affair, Arthur Miller, having divorced Mary Slattery,
married the most celebrated screen star of the day, Marilyn
Monroe: within four years the marriage had turned sour, as
most observers had prophesied. Miller had already continued
his success with *A View From the Bridge* (1955): but his marriage
with the vivacious, glamorous and rising star seemed to distract
and disturb: unhappiness over their inability to have children,
and much else, produced tensions and frictions which resulted
in their eventual separation and divorce. In 1962 Marilyn Monroe died wretchedly, apparently from excess of drink and drugs:
by then Arthur Miller had disentangled himself honourably
from the McCarthyite 'Un-American' smear, had remarried,
and had resumed playwriting (*After the Fall*, 1964; *Incident at
Vichy*, 1964; *The Price*, 1968) and apart from critical introduc-
tions to his plays, had written deeply on dramatic and allied
themes.

Included among his works are listed twelve articles of prose
fiction, including collected short stories, and nearly forty pub-
lished essays and interviews. Several early plays have been successfully filmed, such as *All My Sons* (1948), *Death of a Salesman*
(1952) and *The Crucible*, under the title of *The Witches of Salem*
(1957). More recently other plays, on a variety of themes, have
been written and staged, such as *The American Clock* (1980),
Playing for Time (1981), *Two Way Mirror* (1985) and *The Arch-
bishop's Ceiling* (1989). Arthur Miller's detailed autobiography
Time Bends appeared in 1987: a skilful, candid, meditative personal history which explores his feelings about and motives

behind his experiences and writings. His plays have been extensively translated and performed world-wide; he travels widely, frequently broadcasting on radio and television, especially on American political and cultural topics and trends. He remains a respected tradition and a considerable force in the annals of theatre.

The Crucible in its time

McCarthyism and Arthur Miller

It has sometimes been assumed that *The Crucible* emerged directly and solely from the McCarthy hysteria of the USA in the 1950s: this is untrue, for Miller had long been fascinated by the witch-trials of Puritan Massachusetts in the seventeenth century. But there is equally no doubt that 'McCarthyism', as it came to be called, resurrected his interests and directed them to a dramatic gesture, especially when he became personally involved. A little generalized background information may thus be useful.

The nuclear destruction of Hiroshima and Nagasaki by US personnel ended World War II: but the fateful decision to use atomic power was not taken by the war-time leaders President Roosevelt (who had died in office) or Winston Churchill (who had been voted out of office by a general election), but by a new President of the USA, Harry S. Truman, and a new British Prime Minister, Clement Attlee. Yet one dominant Allied war-time leader remained in great power, Josef Stalin, the stern ruler of the USSR, a country which emerged from the war still incredibly powerful despite its huge losses of men and *matériel*, and which had added largely to its territory and influence in Eastern Europe. The 'Iron Curtain' had come down; by 1949 the USSR exploded an atomic device, and in 1953 its first hydrogen bomb: American nuclear superiority was broken. The 'balance of power' had become a balance of terror, and USA–USSR rivalry and suspicion became intense and nightmarish. In scattered sensitive areas of the world, Berlin, Persia, S.E. Asia, the Mediterranean, Turkey, Greece, Asia itself (among other places), hostility and tensions became polarized as issues in which the USA or the USSR assumed extreme and opposite power pressures and tactics, a situation which has since become summarized as The Cold War. The 'Hot' one would be a matter of sudden annihilation of great tracts of the world, and the first to move, the one with the first 'finger on the button' stood a reasonable chance of becoming the victor. Small local conflicts, backed by one or other of the antagonistic powers, could easily 'escalate' into full-scale nuclear confrontation, despite the United Nations Organisation which itself had settled into 'power blocks', with the larger units, such as the USSR and USA, having a right of veto, the right of denying effective and specific action on the part of other member-states.

In this situation the Korean War broke out in June 1950: the details can be readily discovered from any up-to-date reference book. The essential issue became one of United Nations troops, largely American, opposing the spread of Chinese Communism into S.E. Asia. This was a war of appalling ferocity and staggering human sacrifice, ending in stalemate and frustration. Communism seemed successfully on the move, and American arms, which had proved so overpowering and decisive during the European war, had failed to secure a clear-cut decisive victory. In this atmosphere of national fears and alarms emerged Joseph Raymond MacCarthy (1909–57) a United States Republican Senator. The Cold War, and the Korean upset, demanded that the State system be based on loyal Americanism, and several programmes were authorized to check State employees for their political 'purity'. There were strong fears of Communist infiltration into major State departments, which were heightened when an ex-official of the State Department itself, Alger Hiss, was accused of being a Communist and a spy for the Russians. In England a distinguished atomic physicist, Klaus Fuchs, was found guilty of passing atomic secrets to the Russians. The build-up of fear and suspicion shattered American self-confidence, and played on its conscience: at this opportune moment Senator McCarthy made a speech claiming that the State Department was full of Communists or their 'fellow-traveller' sympathizers, and he found wide support in a merciless campaign against Communism and treachery. As Chairman of the Senate Committee on Government Operations, he smeared with outspoken and often violent vilification the characters of many civil servants, school and university teachers, trades union officials, members of religious minorities, reformers and activists of all kinds. Any or all age-old, youthful flirtation with left-wing thinking, however remote or scanty, was ruthlessly exposed and cynically exaggerated. Many fine reputations could not stand up against the ferocity of this 'smear' campaign, bringing the country to a state of nervous hysteria as it pursued a vicious and merciless 'witch-hunt' of suspected left-wing influence. But when some of the proceedings were televised, and for the first time the American people could see the sneering, bullying, obviously fanatical and unfair handling of evidence by McCarthy in person, public opinion and common sense secured his downfall. The end of the Korean War in 1953 had made it inevitable: his own revealed personality did the rest. McCarthy died in 1957 in unmourned obscurity: his cult was dismissed as 'McCarthywasm' – but not before Arthur Miller had felt the lash. He had watched the near-lunatic state of the nation with growing fear and concern, some of which he expressed in his introduction to the Collected Edition of his plays.

'New sins were being created monthly.'

'There was a sadism here that was breathtaking.'

'I saw accepted the notion that conscience was no longer a private matter but one of state administration. I saw men handing conscience to other men and thanking other men for the opportunity of doing so.'

'The sin of public terror is that it divests man of conscience of himself.'

And when he had himself come under suspicion:

'... a cause ... carried forward by such manifestly ridiculous men, should be capable of paralysing thought itself. It was as though the whole country had been born anew, without a memory even of certain elemental decencies which a year or two earlier no one would have imagined could be altered, let alone forgotten. Astounded, I watched men pass me by without a nod whom I had known rather well for years. ... That so interior and subjective an emotion could have been so manifestly created from without was a marvel to me.'

Arthur Miller fell foul of the House Un-American Activities Committee as it pursued 'subversives': his background was, as we might say today, thoroughly 'screened'. It was discovered that in the thirties Miller had shown interest in Marxism, and was left of centre during the 1940s. In 1947, as a writer, he had attended several meetings of Communist writers in New York; he had sponsored a world youth festival in Prague, and had protested, as a matter of conscience, against the outlawry of the Communist Party. On such grounds, indeed, he had already been refused a passport to visit Brussels. All this amounted to very little indeed: but in the reigning climate of opinion, it was more than enough. Miller was asked to apologize publicly for his 'past relationships': he refused, in disgust and anger. As he then wrote:

'I told the Board that I was not going to genuflect to any newspapermen or howling mob. My attitudes to dictatorship, Nazi and Communist, had been established by my essays. I'd signed the customary loyalty oath when obtaining my passport. I was not going to submit myself to any political means test to practise the profession of letters in the United States.'

It was a brave stand, which only incensed and infuriated the Committee, who, like the prosecutors of the play, were convinced of their being the only judges of what constituted right and wrong. Arthur Miller made a brief appearance before the House Committee in Washington, defending, as he said, not Communists, but the right of an author to write creative literature free from outside pressures. He refused to repent and was sent for trial: he was then found guilty of contempt of court, was fined $500 and given a suspended prison sentence. Miller was not concerned over the money or the sentence: like Proctor, what mattered was his name and his principles; he was determined to have the verdict reversed, and a year later appealed: a court acquitted him completely, shortly before the opening of *The Crucible* (1953).

'The decision has made the long struggle of the past few years fully worthwhile ... I can only hope that the decision will make some small contribution towards eliminating the excesses of congressional activities, and particularly towards stopping the inhuman practice of making witnesses inform on long past friends and acquaintances.'

Thus Arthur Miller had asserted and maintained his identity, and his moral and artistic stature: and above all, his integrity, beyond court decisions. He had lived and seen through something of the spirit and agony of his creation John Proctor, tested in the burning crucible of humanity's fight against evil and its passions.

Puritanism and the Pilgrim Fathers

Readers of Shakespeare's *Twelfth Night* will remember the court-steward Malvolio (whose name means 'wishing-ill') and how he was 'most notoriously abused': tricked over his vanity and treated as a madman. Each of his taunters finds reasons for what would otherwise have been a most cruel streak in their natures — in, admittedly, a rough and cruel society — by accusing Malvolio of Puritanism. Because he is a sober, respected, faithful, dutiful and trusted servant, he is suspect. One says of him: 'Sometimes he is a kind of Puritan'; another bases his dislike because Malvolio brought him out of favour with the lady of the house 'about a bear-baiting here'. He is upbraided thus by Sir Toby – a drunkard and a sponger: 'Dost thou think, because thou art virtuous, there shall be no more cakes and ale?'; and, in the 'joke' that went too far, he is suspected of being possessed by the Devil and bewitched.

Thus, by Shakespeare's time (1564–1616) the term 'Puritan' had become one of derision if not contempt: Lord Macaulay (1800–59) in his *History of England* comments, perhaps unfairly, that: 'The Puritan hated bearbaiting, not because it gave pain to the bear, but because it gave pleasure to the spectator.' They wanted, indeed, to purge, purify, the established church system from all 'popish' abuses. They acknowledged the sole authority of the 'pure Word of God' without 'note or comment': their motto was: 'The Bible, the whole Bible, and nothing but the Bible.' They were serious and high-minded, and tried, especially under the puritanical influence of Oliver Cromwell and his Roundheads, to change many of the social habits and customs of the English people. Sin was crime, and crime was sin: everyone was collectively responsible for sin. The Mosaic Law of the Old Testament was their basis for remodelling the laws of England: adultery was to be punished by death (the very severity of the punishment usually caused local juries to pass the verdict of Not Guilty); drunkenness, swearing and gambling were subject to penalties; Christmas was to be celebrated as a fast day, and not as one allowing 'liberty to carnal and sensual delights', and eventually it was forbidden to observe Easter, Whitsuntide and other festivals. The observance of the Sabbath, legislated under three Acts, was strict and detailed: there was to be no sport or pastime, no work of any kind, no buying or selling, no unnecessary domestic labours, and no travelling by land or water.

Worldly vanities of all kinds were condemned: long hair, the wearing of wigs, the use of cosmetics, ostentatious costume were all denounced; and the Puritans forbade most amusements, entirely of course on Sundays, and extensively wherever possible. Eventually the burden proved too much for most Englishmen to bear: the ordinary citizen's habits were opposed to such fundamental radical changes, and the repressive legislation proved unpopular and unworkable: the Puritans had defeated their own ends. 'Let religion alone; give me my small liberty' had by 1660 become the cry of most Englishmen. The Puritan attempt to enforce strict morality had rebounded, and many zealots abandoned England for the continent and North America (a British colony) because of religious persecution. The Englishman's answer to the fanatical reformers was summed up indeed in that question of Sir Toby to Malvolio: 'Dost thou think, because thou art virtuous, there shall be no more cakes and ale?'

Puritanism had not entirely failed in many ways: undoubtedly there was a social and moral gain: nature was loved the more as showing God's grandeur and handiwork: there were refinements of music and in such language as of Milton and Bunyan: the social bond, the community and family, gained in self-respect and status, and an improvement in intellectual honesty, in simple practical faith, was no bad legacy. But the atmosphere of intolerance, bigotry, self-love, a 'holier-than-thou' attitude was also apparent and long-lasting. Certainly the persecuted minority, who sought refuge overseas, carried with them the best and the worst of these elements. Certainly the bigotry and intolerance, in the name and under the banner of a strict and disciplined religion, carried with them the seeds of their own destruction.

Thus were the New England colonies, the original States of the USA, founded on escape from religious persecution. In 1620 a group of Puritans, later to be known as the Pilgrim Fathers, landed at Plymouth Rock, in what is now Massachusetts, the Old Colony State, having sailed on the *Mayflower*. Seventy-four men and twenty-eight women sought freedom of worship by flight and colonization into a hostile, Indian-harried land. Other colonists followed. The town of Salem, the locality of our play, was founded in 1626 as a commercial venture, and is thus one of the oldest in New England. The name was probably derived from Psalms lxxvi, 2: 'In Salem also is his tabernacle, and his dwelling place in Zion'; and when Arthur Miller went there to consult the city's archives he doubtless saw some of its preserved memorials too: two old burial grounds of 1637 and 1655, and the 'witch house' in which Jonathan Corwin was said to have opened the preliminary examinations of the witchcraft trials of 1692.

The records are clear. Before 1692 there had been forty-four cases of witchcraft and three subsequent hangings in Massachusetts; and in 1688 there had been a sensational case in which some old man was hanged after torture. The Reverend Cotton Mather (1633–1728) had taken part in these trials and had written a tract on the effects of witchcraft, showing how these 'possessed' victims were expected to behave – a great deal was like the more celebrated *Malleus Maleficarum* of 1486 (see Notes, p. 21). This account fell into the hands of a group of young Salem girls, who had fallen under the spell of Tituba, the West Indian slave of the Reverend Samuel Parris: they included Betty aged nine and Parris's niece Abigail Williams aged twelve, girls who clearly missed motherly affection and family security: they found solace with Tituba, who was fond of them, and told them strange tales of her native Barbados and its voodoo-cult, and told their fortunes as they joined her in her kitchen: they made a 'witch-cake', and the imagined power of Tituba (who was unique in the community as the only negro slave-servant) obviously stirred their emotions. One girl, indeed, (Betty in our book) had hysterical fits – not unknown among girls at early adolescence – and, according to Cotton Mather's tract, everything was too clear: it was the work of witchcraft, The Devil was alive in Salem.

Such, certainly, was Parris's conclusion. Tituba was isolated in an outhouse, stripped, tied, flogged without mercy: the girls were terrified by her screams – possibly a foretaste of what they would suffer if the truth came out about their own wickedness in dabbling in the occult – and the slave, to save her skin, confessed to what everyone expected to hear. She had been involved in Devil-worship: and Parris applied the code of the *Malleus Maleficarum*. If she did not fully admit, she would be beaten until she did, tortured and whipped repeatedly. She 'confessed' and implicated others with the first names that came into her head. It became the girls' duty (evidence from the young was always considered particularly strong) to locate and root out the Devil's own and they revelled in the unusual attention paid to them: attention, near-reverence, and fear. They put on cunning performances of demoniacal possession, and obliged their hearers with fanciful details. For her part, Tituba was arrested: but the deadly spark had been lit.

Abigail Williams and her friends became the centre of what seems now to have been a fantastic and sensational witch-hunt. They repeated their performances with all the exhibitionism of frustrated adolescents, doubtless with as much fun as fear Abigail carefully instructing the others in the accepted methods, fully realizing their terrible power. The news spread: panic gripped the whole countryside. More witches were 'discovered',

such as Sarah Good and Sarah Osbourne. Truth to tell, Sarah
Good was a local outcast who slept in barns and begged her way:
the Puritans had no pity for such. Their misery was of God's
inscrutable will, their poverty was part of God's unquestionable
decree, and had to be borne as such. And Sarah Osbourne had
lived in sin with William Osbourne before marriage, and had
been neglectful of proper church attendance. Enough was
enough. A Special Court was appointed, with public meetings in
the church, the Meeting House, the most suitable place for
God's work to be done. The whole proceedings have a wild
bizarre touch strange to the modern reader: but it must be
remembered that many of those involved were by no means
expert lawyers at sifting evidence, and most were genuinely
terrified. The girls performed as the 'witches' were summoned:
when Good and Osbourne, in their innocence, denied all
charges, the girls screamed in demoniac ecstasy. Tituba confessed to her spells with all the slave's age-long mentality of
submission: 'trouble in this house eventually lands on her back',
but she did not give the girls away. She had covenanted with the
Devil indeed, and nine more names had been shown to her in
the Devil's book. But Tituba was illiterate, so the girls' own
methods of detection would suffice. Abigail wiped off old scores:
people were accused or implicated in fantastic tales. The terror
grew with the fantasy. She accused a Martha Cory of suckling a
yellow bird between her fingers: another was a witch because
some butter she had given to a sailor had turned rancid.

The gaols were crowded. Hideous tortures were perpetrated
on those who would not confess. They were stripped naked,
forced to sit cross-legged, long pins were driven into them to
locate the 'Devil's mark': other barbaric methods included star-
vation, denial of sleep, being forced into positions of cramp,
especially with their neck tied to their heels. Some tortures were
unspeakably damaging, physically and mentally. (Consider the
state of Proctor). The girls maintained themselves as the centre
of all this hideous activity, continuing their performances amid
what must seem a wave of lunacy.

A few sane voices protested, even that of Cotton Mather
himself. But the witch-hunt frenzy continued to stalk the land.
The court was on the side of the girls. Abigail even accused the
Reverend George Burroughs, a previous, and unpopular minister of Salem as a main instigator of the witch-cult, and of having

murdered two of his wives. In an atmosphere of frenzy, with the girls keeping up their accusing antics, the authorities tried the victims, some of whom, despite their hazardous condition, openly laughed at the whole folly. Nineteen were hanged. Giles Cory was pressed to death for refusing to plead. Some were defiant upon the very scaffold. When the Reverend Nicholas Noyes asked Sarah Good to save her soul, her resolute answer was 'You're a liar!', and that if she were hanged God would give him blood to drink. She was hanged: ironically, Noyes later died of a haemorrhage. The Reverend Burroughs was also hanged, and so were others, throughout the summer, in public view, before women and children, Abigail and her consorts.

But there came a sudden revulsion. Some of the new intended victims were pious, respectable, prominent merchants: some of the accusations were too wild and extravagant. The court was dissolved on 12 October 1692; all prisoners were released, and the whole contemptible affair became discredited and quickly, ashamedly, pushed out of mind, as far as this was possible. Arthur Miller's own postscript, 'Echoes Down the Corridor' sums up the grisly historical narrative.

Such was the raw material of The Crucible. Patches were amended here and there, some ages changed, some characters combined into one: but a careful reader will see how the essential historical details are incorporated into the play from the contemporary records, always bearing in mind Miller's own prefatory note on the play's historical accuracy. Perhaps against the more recent background of American McCarthyism and European political and religious persecution, the fanaticism of Salem in 1692 becomes, paradoxically, the more credible and the more horrifying in a confused world where essential human freedoms continue to be rigorously denied.

Witchcraft

There was, fundamentally, nothing remarkable in this belief in witchcraft. Puritanism was based on the divinity of the Bible: as Proctor says: '. . . the Bible speaks of witches, and I will not deny them'. The King James's Authorized Version of the Bible (1611) contains the stern Mosaic injunction: 'Thou shalt not suffer sorcerers to live.' Satan, the fallen Archangel who sought to rival God, and thus the Antichrist, the leader of the legions of devils, is mentioned over forty times; as the 'Adversary' twenty more times. Devils and demons are to be found in over fifty references: witches and witchcraft are specifically mentioned. English laws against witches had indeed preceded this translation of the Bible into common speech, for such statutes against witches had been known since King Canute's day: and James I himself had written his *Daemonologie* demonstrating the reality of witches.

Yet the notion of women being in league with demons goes back to prehistoric fertility cults and rituals, and had developed and diversified strongly through pagan into religious eras. It was considered a heresy, and indeed became a convenient religious and political scapegoat. Endless statutes, especially throughout the Reformation era, defined the evil and prescribed suitable punishments, and the seventeenth century saw the highest number of trials in Europe. The last recorded conviction in England was in 1712, although as late as 1722 a woman was actually burned as a witch in Sunderland.

But when the belief was widespread, even among the most highly educated, the victims (some three hundred thousand in Europe between 1484 and 1782) suffered trial, torture of unspeakable cruelty, and death. Scholars accepted it: a papal Bull of 1484 gave witch-hunts and witch-hunters full authority and the cruellest powers of suppression and eradication. The *Malleus Maleficarum*, written by two Dominican Inquisitors, appeared in 1486: it is the oldest and the most successful of all handbooks on European witchcraft. Detailed and practical, buttressed with innumerable references to countless authorities, it moves logically and mercilessly through all aspects of sorcery and heresy, recommends the crucial tests and proofs of the Evil Eye, magical spells, fortune-telling and other methods of divination, astrology and charms, incubi and succubi, and countless other demons and similar devils and their manifestations: 'We dare not refrain from enquiring into them lest we imperil our own salvation', as the authors say.

However obscure the origins and causes; however remote the idea of witchcraft may appear to us (perhaps our own ideas stem mainly from Shakespeare's *Macbeth* as much as Walt Disney's tall-hatted broomstick-riding cackling hags) witchcraft was real enough throughout Europe and, through Puritan colonization, in North America too into what may loosely be called the

Renaissance and immediate post-Renaissance period. Local misfortunes, especially in remote and scattered mountain or pastoral regions; fire, famine and flood, unexpected crop failures and unusual deaths (especially of children – hence midwives were especially suspect), adverse sickness among people or cattle: these and countless other apparently inexplicable phenomena needed a cause, and a scapegoat on which revengeful blame could be heaped. If the occasion could be turned to wipe off some old scores, perhaps involve some otherwise inaccessible gain, then some neighbour of unusual or eccentric personality, perhaps physically or mentally disordered, some old mumbling crone, who had outlived her usefulness to the community and her own vigour could fall foul of rumour, wild superstition, and the malevolent or mean. The Bible proscribed them: the ancient Church had legislated against them; and the believers believed.

The people of Salem believed well enough in the Devil and his works: it was not in this that they were hypocritical. It was the ultimate blend of heresy and sorcery – both religious evils, and was thus the greatest adversary of their theocracy, or God-governed state. That the witch-hunt could have been inspired by a few frustrated adolescent girls, pursued to extremes by those who wished to gain materially from its side-effects, and its relentlessly exacting judicial murder, if not martyr-like sacrifice – *that* is the ultimate essence of human folly and error Miller wants his audiences to feel, and see purged out, burnt out, of the white-hot crucible. They could not see that they were doing a far greater wrong than anything they were legally, and religiously, condemning. Only by increase of death and false condemnation – and what could be more wrong and truly evil? – did they feel they were doing the only right thing. They were blind to their own hideous, monstrous, superlatively virtuous and self-centred immorality. Man's inhumanity to man, especially in the name of religion, liberty, equality, or what you will, is the supreme yet apparently eternal paradox of human history.

Miller's conception of drama

When Arthur Miller, as an undergraduate of the University of Michigan, first entered for a drama competition – with his first ever play, written in six days (a competition which he won), he had seen only two plays in his life and read only three others. He did not even know how long a typical act took on the stage, and had to ask a fellow student's advice on this.

It is, however, quite clear that by the time he wrote *The Crucible* (1953) and indeed, by the date of his earliest successful stage play (*All My Sons*, 1947), he had become a considerable craftsman, wielding a remarkable intellect, in the business of playwriting. Ten years later, the New York edition of his *Collected Plays* contained an illuminating introduction, essential reading for any earnest student of Miller's view and techniques of drama. A few self-explanatory extracts follow:

A play, I think, ought to make sense to common sense people.

Drama is akin to the other inventions of man in that it ought to help us to know more, and not merely to spend our feelings.

Drama . . . must represent a well-defined expression of profound social needs, needs which transcend any particular form of society or any particular historic moment. I take it that if one could know enough about a human being one could discover some conflict, some value, some challenge, however major or minor, which he cannot find it in himself to walk away from or turn his back on. (A play) . . . is part of the present tense par excellence. . . . the lasting appeal of tragedy is due to our need to face the fact of death in order to strengthen ourselves for life.

Nobody wants to be a hero . . . but in every man there is something he cannot give up and still remain himself – a core, an identity, a thing that is summed up for him by the sound of his own name on his own ears. If he gives that up, he becomes a different man, not himself.

The direct relevance of most of this to *The Crucible* is abundantly clear, and while many of these ideas relate to the whole body of his playwriting, we shall consider them and other factors solely in relation to this one play.

It must first of all be realized firmly that a play in a theatre is a distinctive and unique affair: even if, by modern techniques it is perfectly filmed and recorded, the re-run performance would become transposed into a film, and lose its immediacy, stage-perspective and intimacy of the live theatre original. Among the literary arts themselves a play is also unique in this immediate appeal to all the senses of an alert audience: they cannot halt or slow down its movement as in book form they can turn back some pages to refresh the memory or check an allusion, or give the mind pause to make interim judgements of particular episodes: and only by leaving the theatre before the full performance can they parallel putting back an unfinished book on its shelf. A successful serious play, therefore, has to have impact – of character, language and situation, sharp purpose and clear design. It must grasp its audience, involve it, rapidly, and not let it go until its actions have been played out, though it can vary the pressures and moods along the way. The audience must be mentally, sometimes almost spiritually involved in an act of participation: its credulity must not be strained, nor its conscience flattered or outraged. Its characters must move understandably in an understandable however unlovely world, and they must act naturally, typically, once given their individuality. The play as a whole must communicate, even the incommunicable: it must cross the footlights at some point over to the minds and conscience of the audience.

Miller's characterization, style and language will be considered separately: but above all these things though served by them, his view of drama is more important. The play must be immediate in its appeal to reasonably intelligent people, who must also see that, as in all worthwhile literature, the play is something larger than the sum of its parts, larger in a sense than itself, something beyond itself. It is in and of society: it is 'committed'. It may well shed light on a particular place in a particular time (say, Salem in 1692), but it must reach beyond these and present a *universal* message.

Comparison of plays and playwrights is almost always dangerous in its over-simplifying and over-generalization; but without for a moment comparing Miller and Shakespeare it must be obvious to a reader of, say *The Merchant of Venice, Twelfth Night*, or *Othello* (a few of many possible examples) that the setting of Venice, Illyria or Cyprus is almost irrelevant: the place is only marginally important to the central theme. In its own way each is a play in an Elizabethan English situation, with references and topical allusions immediately understandable only to an English Elizabethan audience. Yet it is equally obvious that the situation of Shylock, Viola or Othello is not a local or limited one, but a universal theme of, say, alien hostility, love, or jealousy. The situations are eternal.

So it is with *The Crucible*. The Salem of 1692 could be the France of the Terror, Germany or Italy of the 1930s, the USSR of the 1940s or the USA of the 1950s; or anywhere, anytime, given the forces of collective intolerance and the machinery of judicial terror. The past is the present which is also the future, in social and human terms.

Even beyond this, Miller is preoccupied with the human condition in society: so, of course, are most serious writers. But Miller has always confined himself to tragedy in a special atmosphere, that of the victim in a false society. This society is, sometimes unwittingly, sometimes knowingly, destructive and evil. The supreme authority of a state can become an active relentless persecutor, and truth can be preserved and proved only by some victims' isolation and death. What counts for Miller is a realization of one's personal integrity, and an affirmation of a personal, positive responsibility within a society. Most of us, willynilly, are the passive accepting sheep (remember their role in Orwell's *Animal Farm*): we comply with society, with authority: it is cosier and less troublesome that way; we accept and condone what seems to be the national will, whatever that is – and it may change from time to time. But for some man, rightly or wrongly, there comes a moment of truth, when an issue of clear principle, honestly and sincerely held, becomes endangered; a moment when one cannot put off the responsibility on someone else's shoulder, when one's whole conscience is at stake. For these, death, martyr-like perhaps – but arousing more pride than sorrow – is the only worthwhile gesture left. This is the essence of Miller's whole theatrical view, and it is worked out in some detail in *The Crucible*.

Act summaries, critical commentary, textual notes and revision questions

Analysis of Miller's commentary

Act 1 (An Overture)

Early one sunny spring morning in 1692, in Salem, Massachusetts, Betty, the ten-year-old daughter of the widower Reverend Samuel Parris is lying motionless in a trance-like sleep. Apparently she and some other local girls have been encouraging Parris's Barbadian servant Tituba to raise spells, and Parris surprised them while they were dancing in the forest: some of them may have been naked. All of them, certainly, are likely to be severely punished if and when the truth emerges. One of these girls is Parris's niece, Abigail Williams, who will admit only to the dancing: but she reports a rumour of witchcraft, and some townsfolk have called upon their priest – are in fact meeting there and then downstairs in their concern: Parris, who has made many enemies for various reasons during his ministry, is pathetically clutching at straws trying to convince himself that no such terrible evil as witchcraft has entered and befallen his house.

No sympathy indeed comes from two of his callers, Mr and Mrs Putnam. The man is a noted landgrabber, constantly running to law, always in dispute with his neighbours; the wife, who has lost seven children at or near birth, and whose own daughter Ruth has been acting queerly, takes it for granted – both are quite convinced – that witchcraft is at the root of it all.

Others girls come in: Mercy Lewis, the Putnams' servant, and Mary Warren, the servant of farmer John Proctor. When they are left alone for a short while it becomes clear from their conversation that they are ruled and exploited somewhat by Abigail Williams. Betty revives a little in this company of her own age, but is still nervous and slightly hysterical about their trying to conjure spirits and drinking charms: indeed, Abigail has drunk one specifically to kill Proctor's wife Elizabeth – but the girl threatens them violently with unspecified punishment if any reveals more than their minor follies.

Then John Proctor arrives: respectable, respected and forthright. All leave except the still-suffering Betty and the attractive Abigail, and it is revealed that these two, the married man and the cunning, ruthlessly powerful yet physically attractive Abigail have known sexual intimacy: it is also clear that Abigail has set her sights upon winning over Proctor completely by any means, but that he – whose ailing wife bundled out Abigail, her ex-servant, into the street once the situation became clear – looks upon the girl as a child, with mingled shame and sympathy. When Abigail blackens Elizabeth's name, Proctor reacts sharply.

Rebecca Nurse, a very old and highly-respected woman comes in, and thinks that the whole affair is a silly childish prank of adolescents, which will soon run itself out if left alone: but Mr and Mrs Putnam cling tenaciously to their belief in witchcraft. In the course of discussion, Proctor accuses Parris of keeping folk away from their church-going by his constant preaching about hell-fire and damnation: as he turns to go, having work to do on his homestead, and shrugging off a typical accusation of Mr Putnam involving bounds and property, the Reverend Mr Hale enters.

Hale is an acknowledged expert in the specialised field of witchcraft, with skill in its detection and expulsion. He listens carefully to all the available evidence so far produced or admitted, examines Betty, and talks cleverly and passionately about the strength and power of the Devil. Proctor has already left, hoping that Hale's influence will be on the side of sanity and reason.

Abigail and Tituba are questioned particularly closely over the forest incident: Abigail is pressed hard, almost to the point of confession over the charm; Tituba, more easily cowed, and by her origins more susceptible to strong religious feelings, admits to producing charms when so requested by the girls: she is so frightened that she asserts a belief in witches, and names some of those people in Salem whom she believes the Devil works through or has contacted, to Parris's horror. Abigail takes this scapegoat opportunity, now that the major danger to herself has been relieved, of assuming a state of vision and confession. She names other folk in league with the Devil, and, by some hysterical fascinated imitation, Betty and Abigail pour out a string of names, and the curtain falls on their harrowing, condemning cries.

Salem City and county seat of Essex County, Massachusetts, USA, on the North coast of Massachusetts Bay, 15 miles N.E. of Boston. Founded in 1626, it is the oldest town of the State. (See Notes, p. 17.)

Meeting (*Meetings) prayer-meetings.
Shovelboard now called shove-halfpenny: a game played by pushing disks or coins along a smooth board marked with transverse lines. One can readily gamble on the scoring system.
Persecuted in England (See Notes, p.16.)
Jamestown Named, of course, after James I, this was a town of Virginia, the first permanent English settlement in America. It was founded in 1607. The site is preserved as a historical relic.
Virginia One of the thirteen original states of the USA, named after Elizabeth I, 'The Virgin Queen' of England James I granted its original charter: it became a crown colony in 1624, seceding with the southern states in 1861. Here slavery began in the original thirteen states and on this basis it became a rich tobacco-plantation state.
Mayflower (See Notes, p.17.)
The Times ... out of joint See Shakespeare's *Hamlet*, end of Act I, Scene V.
Lucifer Name attached to Satan, the fallen archangel (as in Milton's *Paradise Lost*) and thus to the Devil as the principle of evil.

Barbados Most easterly of the West Indian Islands, first settled by the English in 1627.
hearty fit and well.

*variant reading in Heinemann edition

Beverly A town of Essex County, Massachusetts, situated on an inlet of the Atlantic opposite Salem.

Goody Proctor 'Goody' was short for 'Goodwife' (the feminine of 'Goodman') and was used as a title, among religious and agricultural communities, for the mistress of the household.

Forked and Hoofed Like the Devil, usually represented in medieval times with a cloven foot and a forked tail. The origins of this representation are obscure and much debated.

Narragansett On Rhode Island, the smallest of the states of the USA, settled in the sixteenth century. All the early colonists and pioneers had naturally to contend with and defend their occupation from the local American-Indian tribes. There is a suggestion here, too, of the strength of the 'ex-serviceman' group (called 'veterans' in the USA): many of these rallied fervently to the patriotic calls of Senator McCarthy. (See Notes, p.13.)

unbaptized because they had not lived long enough for the religious, ceremonial 'bathing'.

sucking mouth She is wasting away as if some devilish influence is draining her life away, preying upon her.

Boston Capital city of Massachusetts, first settled in 1630 by Puritans: the name came from the English town of Boston in Lincolnshire whence many of its original settlers emigrated.

pointy Sharp.

reddish bloody.

posh Exclamation of derision and impatience.

'going up to Jesus' No true psalm can contain a reference to Jesus, and indeed there were very few hymns in use before 1696: while the phrase is untraceable, the dramatic effect is sound.

Wardens Churchwardens, the principal officers of the church.

Harvard College Founded in 1636 and named after John Harvard (1607–38) an English emigrant to Massachusetts who left much of his fortune and library to found the college.

Quakers Members of the Society of Friends, founded in the middle of the seventeenth century, with no definite creed and no regular ministry.

Inquisition A court set up to inquire into offences against Roman Catholicism, fully established by 1229. The Dominican Order of monks were the general administrators, and used torture to obtain recantations. It was particularly active in Spain.

Old boy The Devil, familiarly and jocularly.

Luther Martin Luther (1483–1546), German religious reformer who became the founder of what may be called 'Protestant Civilization' by denouncing the Papacy. He survived a trial for heresy and excommunication for his challenge to orthodoxy.

Erasmus Desiderius Erasmus (1466–1536), Dutch scholar and theologian: a great humanist.

succubi Devils supposed to assume a female body to consort with men in their sleep. Here, more of a fearsome diabolical 'nightmare' of a belief.

Red Hell Soviet Communist ideology.

klatsches (**klatches*). The general meaning of this German word is 'gossip', 'tittle-tattle', 'scandal-mongering'. The use here would suggest that this could have been the immediate, but not the only or final reason, for the secret meetings.

Dionysiac Of Dionysus, the Greek precursor of the Roman Bacchus. The nocturnal festivals in his honour were apparently characterized by drunkenness, debauchery, and general licentiousness to the point of orgy.

American baptist The Baptists are a Protestant sect, with immersion of the body in water (for adults and children) as a fundamental principle, symbolizing the washing away of sin, and their spirituality and adherence to Scripture. In the USA they are the largest of the Protestant groups: in Rhode Island in the seventeenth century there was established the first modern state in which the control of religious matters was taken entirely out of the hands of the civil government by the Baptist church.

Incubi The masculine equivalent of 'succubi' above: used also of a nightmare in general.

In nomine Domini Sabaoth sui filiique ite ad infernos The Latin may be thus translated: 'In the name of the Lord of Hosts, and of his son, go to the infernal spirits.'

kettle Cooking pot.

truck Meddle; bargain.

Revision questions on Act 1

1 Summarize what you have understood so far in this Act about the characters of (a) Reverend Parris, (b) Mr Putnam, (c) John Proctor, and (d) Abigail Williams.

2 Why is Betty so afflicted?

3 Why does Abigail lie about their 'dancing like a heathen' in the forest?

4 What is Rebecca Nurse's opinion of the girl's escapade? What does she recommend? Why does no one take much notice of this?

5 What can we assume about Reverend Hale's character from his conversations, *not* from Miller's supplied commentary?

6 Why did Abigail and the girls begin to accuse Salem townsfolk of witchcraft? Why is Goody Proctor not named?

7 What physical movements on the stage, and what changes of mood, have you observed to be significant in this Act?

Act 2

Eight days have passed, and John Proctor comes home from seeding his fields. His wife Elizabeth is upstairs with their three children. Proctor flavours the stew cooking on the range more to his liking, and his wife comes down and serves him his meal. There is an atmosphere of strain, estrangement, distance between them. Elizabeth tells him that their servant-girl Mary Warren, now apparently an important witness at the trial proceedings at Salem, has informed her that fourteen people are now imprisoned, and that the girls, led by Abigail, are accusing numbers of people, almost at whim, of witchcraft: and what they say is believed outright. Elizabeth thinks that John ought to go to the court and tell them about Abigail's being a fraud: after all, this was reasonably obvious from their last encounter, when she (Abigail) and John were momentarily alone in Parris's house. There is increased tension now between husband and wife, rooted in Proctor's shame for his moment of adulterous passion and intimacy: for which Abigail was promptly and immediately hustled out of the house by Elizabeth.

Mrs Warren comes in, giving Elizabeth a little rag doll, a poppet; she tells them of how more townsfolk have been condemned to death on the girl's testimony and indictment. Proctor will have none of this devil-talk, and Elizabeth fears strongly that Abigail will soon name her, so that the young girl may have Proctor wholly for herself. This he hotly denies.

At this point the Reverend Hale enters: he questions them guardedly and carefully about the strength of their religious convictions. Proctor openly expresses a personal dislike for Mr Parris: but otherwise seems faithful enough. Yet Hale seems suspicious, and asks him to recite the Ten Commandments. Proctor manages to stumble through them, more or less accurately: but omits, until prompted by Elizabeth – significantly – the

one prohibiting adultery. Elizabeth presses John to tell Hale
what he knows of the real nature of Abigail. Giles Corey and
Francis Nurse appear: both their wives have been taken on
various charges: even Hale regards this as a monstrous injustice.

Ezekiel Cheever arrives on court business: he has a warrant
for Elizabeth, 'named' by Abigail Williams. He asks if she has a
poppet: and the one just given her by Mary Warren in produced. Cheever finds a long needle pushed into it: this is
apparently a very bad omen, and he tells her the story of
Abigail's having been similarly pierced by a needle: clearly the
inference is that Elizabeth has done this to her by devilish asso-
ciation with a 'familiar' spirit. Mary Warren is questioned about
the doll: it turns out that Abigail was sitting alongside when it
was made. But court business has to be done, despite Proctor's
remonstrances and defiance in tearing up the Governor's warrant. Elizabeth decides to yield to the law: she makes some
domestic arrangements, and is chained – again despite Proctor's
violent anger – and led away. Proctor now decides to face the
court, with Mary Warren, and what he knows to be the truth. He
must denounce Abigail openly and publicly, admitting his adultery. His wife's life is at stake: no cost can be too great to save
her. Everything will now depend on his ability to convince the
court that Abigail is no wayward cʰild, and that the whole story
is based on lies and fraud. Everything may have to be exposed
for what it really is: and this truth may be bitter.

poppet Doll.
clapboard Thin boards used in covering wooden houses.
Long needle This sticking of pins or needles into small models was a
relic of the 'sympathetic magic' of classical witchcraft: this was to
provoke comparable results on the living characters they represented,
and is not unknown today in primitive communities in Europe and
Asia.
Familiar spirit Usually called 'familiars', these were low-ranking
demons, generally in the shape of a small domestic animal, advising
the witch and performing small malicious errands: the witches of
Shakespeare's *Macbeth* (I,1) respond to the calls of their familiars: 'I
come, Graymalkin' (a grey cat) and 'Paddock calls' (a toad).
Pontius Pilate The Roman governor of Judaea, AD 26–36, who
ordered the crucifixion of Jesus. See Matthew xxvii, 24.

Revision questions on Act 2

1 What indications are given of the domestic estrangement between John and Elizabeth Proctor: what kind of a wife is she?

2 Outline Mary Warren's part throughout this Act.

3 Why does Mr Hale arrive to question the Proctors? What, in your opinion, does he make of each of them?

4 Why does Proctor dislike Reverend Parris?

5 In your own words, outline the episode of the giving, discovery, and alleged importance of the poppet.

6 What crucial decision does Proctor make at the end of the Act?

Act 3

In the Salem General Court the prosecutor Judge Hathorne is questioning Martha Corey, who protests her complete innocence: her aged husband Giles vigorously asserts that he has evidence of the false nature of the whole affair, and of Putnam's landgrabbing involvement. The Deputy Governor Danforth and the Reverend Parris come in to hear the evidence, such as it is: Martha Corey has been condemned, apparently, because she was always reading books: but the full details will have to wait. Francis Nurse, for his part, protests over the condemnation of his wife and claims that the court has been deceived by the fraudulent activity of the girls: but the judges are and remain convinced of their own infallibility and uprightness.

John Proctor now asserts himself, and tells the court that his servant-girl Mary Warren has signed a deposition to the effect that she has never seen any spirits. Parris, who remains convinced that it must be — it has to be — witchcraft, constantly interrupts, suggesting that Proctor is out to undermine the authority of the court. But Proctor, backed largely by Mr Hale, persists in his case that the whole business is a pretence. He is closely questioned as to his own private spiritual strength, but he presses his case, admitting that he has neither love of nor loyalty to his parish priest Mr Parris, that the proceedings are based on lies.

He is told that there is no need so to plead, for his wife

Elizabeth has pleaded pregnancy: she will be spared until after the birth of her child – giving her, say, a year more of life. He thus is not bound to say more just to defend her: her life is secure at least for a little while. But he refuses to drop his case. He presents a petition: but this is set aside to be used as a list for further arrests for examination and interrogation: the situation is becoming serious. Giles Corey accuses and condemns Putnam as working behind the scenes, accusing Salem folk so that he can buy up their property. Proctor goes back to his plea, firmly and calmly, that Mary Warren has openly confessed to the truth of the whole affair: all the witchcraft element is a lie and a figment of the imagination. The girl is questioned, and admits some of the truth. At this point the four principally involved girls enter: Danforth tells them of Mary's admission, but Abigail denies all of it out of hand. Proctor insists that she is not a child and need not be treated as one: Mary Warren keeps to her story, but then Abigail affects one of her trance-like states, and the hysteria grows. Proctor, to put an end to all this nonsense, pulls Abigail to her feet by her hair, and denounces her as a whore, admitting his adultery. He has sacrificed in open court his name, his integrity, his honour, to prove Abigail's worthlessness. But a sterner test is then arranged. Elizabeth is summoned – the wife who will never lie – and she cannot bring herself to condemn her husband as a lecher: she is quite unaware of what has already happened in court.

Danforth believes this testimony against Proctor and Hale: to emphasize the situation, the girls again go into a visionary state, and under this 'influence' Mary Warren says that Proctor has threatened to murder her if she does not help him to undermine the court's authority and so save his wife. The judges are convinced: Proctor is himself allied to the Devil.

From his wild and tortured mind comes an agonized accusation even against God: he sees the Devil, indeed, all round him. If it is not realized by all sane thinking men that this is a monstrous, dangerous, murdering fraud, then they all deserve condemnation. Hale, at this turn of the proceedings, quits and abandons the court in horror and disgust: Proctor and Giles Corey are led off to prison.

Act 3

Marblehead to Lynn Marblehead is a seaport of Massachusetts, settled by Englishmen in 1629; it is about six miles from Lynn, another seaport.
Raphael . . . Tobias In the book of the Apocrypha, Tobit v, 2–8.
ipso facto By that very fact (Latin)
augur bit Properly 'auger': a boring tool fitted into a carpenter's brace.
I have known her This is a Biblical expression for having had sexual experience of a person.

Revision questions on Act 3

1 What is Parris's role throughout this Act? Are any aspects of it likely to change your original opinion of his character as so far revealed?

2 What is your estimate of Danforth? Is he a sincere man? How can you explain his apparent cruelty?

3 What part does Giles Corey play in this Act?

4 What is the full content of Mary Warren's testimony? What is Abigail's response, and why?

5 At what moment, and why just then, does Proctor reveal his misalliance with Abigail?

6 Why does Hale abandon the court when he does?

7 List all the characters involved in the main court scene, and comment on the testimony and behaviour of each.

Act 4

The Act opens three months later, early on a bitterly cold still-moonlit morning in the autumn of 1692. A dirty, smelly bedraggled pair of prisoners, Tituba and Sarah Good, drunken, confused and excitable, are cleared elsewhere for Deputy-Governor Danforth and Judge Hathorne. The two witch-hunters and major prosecutors talk of the Reverend Hale's constant prayers among the condemned, accompanied by a now worried and distraught Mr Parris. Ezekiel Cheever, still clerk of the court, speaks of the impoverishment, distress and general breakdown of the community through neglect and dispute, a direct result of so much imprisonment. Parris enters with the news that Mr Hale has brought several of the condemned prisoners near to full confessions of their devilish associations, which action could save their lives: he adds the more staggering and significant news that his niece Abigail Williams and one of the girls, Mary Lewis, have run away, after rifling his strong-box and stealing over thirty pounds (a very considerable sum of money in those days). He asks that the hanging of such note-worthy people as Rebecca Nurse and John Proctor should be postponed until, perhaps through Mr Hale's ministrations, they confess. He fears some open rebellion against the court, some-thing already apparently happening in other places: he himself has already had clear warning that his own life is in danger. Danforth resists any postponement.

The Reverend Hale comes in, a broken, sorrowing, tired but determined man, and directly he asks Danforth to pardon the condemned. Danforth refuses. Twelve have already died, seven more are to hang at dawn. This is God's law, and cannot be softened. Now Proctor has not yet been seen by Hale: perhaps the sight of his pregnant wife Elizabeth might incline him to confession: they have, after all, been forcibly separated for three months.

While Elizabeth and John are being fetched, Hale reflects bitterly on the destroyed community, and his own involvement in the devilish conspiracy. When Elizabeth comes in, chained, dishevelled and gaunt, Hale begs her to prevail upon her hus-band to confess. What he confesses to will be a lie: everyone will know that it will be a lie to save his life, forfeit by the hangman's rope at sunrise. But all those condemned are inno-cent: if a lie will save them, then they ought to lie. Faith has turned to blood: a lie, however technically ungodly, might save a life.

Elizabeth agrees to see her husband: and the chained gaol-filthy, tortured Proctor is brought face to face with his wife. They are left alone: and they are nearer in spirit and love than they have ever been. They at first quietly exchange what news there is: of their children, who are being cared for by a neigh-bour; of Giles Corey's terrible but defiant death by being pressed under heavy stones; and of the other victims. Proctor tells her that he is moved to confess, and asks her advice and opinion. But Elizabeth pleads with him to come to his own resolution: to make his own fatal, fateful, crucial decision: and he does. He says he wants to confess, knowing this to be a lie, the greatest lie. The officials cluster, and Proctor tells them that he saw the Devil, and was committed to do his evil works. The sight of Rebecca Nurse, however, unnerves him in his swerving and he becomes adamant in his determination not to involve anyone else. He further refuses to sign the document of confession: he has already sold himself to enough evil in admitting to a lie, but he will not have his name, his honour and his integrity likewise destroyed. Parris and Hale beg and plead that he should commit this last act, just to sign: the alternative is death. Elizabeth, hitherto dry-eyed and calm, weeps hysterically: but Proctor has made his last decision. He realizes that this last stand shows some preserved inner goodness: honour must, even at the cost of one's life, be maintained amid the greatest evil, and is unassailable. He and Rebecca, almost proudly, are led out to death.

A drumroll begins: Elizabeth has the last searing word as the sunlight pours in: at last, Proctor has absolved himself in and through death, and has reached – God willing – a state of eternal goodness.

Act 4

Andover A town of Essex County, Massachusetts on the south-easst side of the Merrimac valley.

Revision questions on Act 4

1 What is the dramatic function of the opening of this Act, up to the entry of the prosecuting judges?

2 What comments are made on the disruption of Salem community life, and by whom?

3 Why, in your opinion, did Abigail and Mary run away?

4 What has apparently been happening in Andover which may affect the course of the Salem witch-trials?

5 Why does Danforth give Proctor another, last, chance?

6 What does Hale want Elizabeth to say or do for her husband? What is her reaction before, and after, Proctor's entry and talk with her?

7 What is the gist of the conversation between Elizabeth and John Proctor?

Arthur Miller's art
in *The Crucible*

Plot, Structure, Characterization and Style are so interrelated, interdependent and tightly interlaced in any profound literary work that there is a danger of the student's coming to believe that if they are treated separately, they can in fact be considered separate and watertight divisions. So long as it is realized that they almost inextricably interweave and overlap, some useful points may be made: they are convenient headings, useful labels for the purposes of closer study. A play, as a poem, must always and eventually be seen and felt as a unity, as a whole composition: some dissection may help to a clearer view of the final wholeness and completeness of the entire work. As the main plot is outlined in sections preceding each Act, it need not be repeated here: under Characterization, after some general ideas, each major character will be considered separately.

Structure

The Plot summary preceding each of the Notes to each Act reveals the broad movement of the play: but Arthur Miller has a sense of the detailed as well as of the total structure, and one or two aspects of this may be found interesting.

Each of the four Acts has an essential unity of place: Parris's home, Proctor's house, the Court Room of the Church, and the prison compound. This is obviously theatrically sound and convenient: the absence of scene-divisions gives each Act its own focus and solidity, and there are no visual distractions of changing scene. Due weight and concentration is thus thrust upon the actor and his words within a specific and uninterrupted setting. Indeed, each opening has a specific theatrical effect. Nothing is said for a little time at the beginning of Acts 1 and 2; there are, however, significant movements, and the audience can attune itself to the scene. Similarly, Act 3 opens on an empty room: but voices are soon heard, and over a dozen lines of varying intensity are spoken before an actor appears. Act 4, too, opens in silence and apparent emptiness, until the shuffling of the drunken warder rouses from the gloom the dismal shapes of the ragged inmates. Thus is each opening 'button-holing': one's attention is immediately riveted: one's senses are expectant. The atmosphere of each Act is made sharply, and remains lingering and strong. The whole story is opened with the frightened daughter of the unloved Parris; the involvement of Proctor with Abigail is intensified by the second Act's delicate and subtle exploration of his relationship with his wife, who, at the end, is taken away as one of the accused through Abigail. The Court scene of Act 3 completes the situation of false accusation and unjust trial: and the closing Act is agonizingly set within the four narrow walls of the horrible chill atmosphere of the prison, from which Proctor is to be led away to his death.

Coupled to this clear purposeful division of the story there is also a symbolic underlining in the effects of light and sunlight, easily managed but nonetheless very impressive in the modern theatre with the auditorium in comparative darkness. In the opening scene the morning sunlight streams into the little room – a little spring light outshining the still-lit candle of the dark hours: they have been darker still for the frightened easily led child and her un-understanding father: at the end, the 'enraptured' Abigail is seen against the lighting 'as though in a pearly light'. Act 2 begins with a view of the fading daylight outside the low dark room of Proctor's home: and much more will fade into darkness until, at the end, Proctor walks out under the open black sky. The bustle of Act 3 begins with sunlight pouring in: metaphorically and symbolically, light is to be thrown on the whole judicial procedure and its gross faults: the closing words of Proctor combine images of blackness and evil, and fire (105/96). There is no light, but for moonlight, at the opening of Act 4: what light is left? The spiritual and mental gloom is deep and unrelenting. But at the end, the terrible and overpowering end, the new sun of the morning pours upon Elizabeth's uplifted face, as Proctor goes defiantly, triumphantly, to a doom he has conquered by suffering, to a light beyond earthly view and comprehension.

The pace and intensity of each Act is worth consideration, for they naturally affect the rhythm of the whole play viewed as a unit. With strong theatrical sense Miller starts each Act, as we have seen, on a soft, often still quiet note: in fact in Acts 1, 2 and 4 there is actual or implied sleeping (Betty on the bed; the Proctor children being put to bed; the prisoners lying in their dirt asleep). Contrast this with the ending of each Act: the ecstatic condemning cries of the frenzied girls (50/*40*); Proctor's cry of horror (75/*66*); Proctor's declaration of faith (105/*96*) and, of course, the agony of Elizabeth's final words (126/*116*).

There is contrast, too, within each Act; moments when actions, words or meanings pile up and accelerate, making little peaks and climaxes. A brief analysis of Act 1 will serve as an example. From the quiet rather slow beginning the pace quickens with the entry of the Putnams (21/*9*) and Ann's witch-ridden convictions; then an even pace reasserts itself until Abigail threatens and John Proctor enters. The tension between them, and later among Parris and the Putnams, maintains itself, bursting out and lifting itself a little in the animated bickering and quarrelling (33–36/*22–26*). Hale's entry marks a new phase, a moment of rest and quiet, although we are now aware of many exposed pressures and tensions underlying words and attitudes: the movement quickens with Hale's questioning of the girls and Tituba, with some strong give and take of dialogue: this itself quickens in speed as the lines shorten in length – a staccato rapidity in the quick-fire 'revelations' (49–5/*39–40*), each one a potential death-blow; the Act ends echoing with the hammered-home climax of accusation. In much the same way Miller controls, although it never seems obviously contrived, a rise and fall within each Act: in Act 2, for example, after long quiet steadying sections, there is a rising rhythm and pace when Proctor resolutely confronts his wife (55/*45*), heightening to a rage with Mary Warren (55/*46*), then continuing on a tenser strain, changed but not really relaxed by the unexpectedness and potential danger of Hale's intrusion: in the ensuing dialogue there are comparable rises and falls of mood and emotion. This interlaced and varying rhythm, this swing and sway of tension and atmosphere, matches the feel of the moment, and is startlingly effective theatre.

Generally, too, Miller keeps things moving. He is good at controlling and managing quite a large cast on and off the stage. Again, Act 1 can be used as a characteristic example: it is worth jotting down the pattern of exits and entrances, seeing how naturally people move in and out, pushing on the plot, developing the characterization and the atmosphere. Note, for example, how Abigail enters and stays while others such as Parris, Susanna, the two Putnams, Proctor, move out to stay out, their function complete for the moment, or return for some specific role. But Abigail remains, hears all, participates, is left with her frightened companions whom she dominates (is that why she chooses to remain?). She is there to confront Proctor, and again remains in the background for some time, saying nothing: but she can react throughout the various encounters until finally, with Tituba, she dominates the scene as the curtain falls. Perhaps Francis Nurse is less well managed, mentioned very early on in Miller's prose commentary in Act1 (31/20) as a respected and influential man, but not introduced into the play until Act 3, when his wife Rebecca has already been condemned (79/69). He has seven lines or so in exchanges; does not speak at all for a long time, and then only with four short lines, has but one short line again after a very long time, and then is heard no more. Apart from maintaining something of the effect of a crowd scene, this may be an oversight to keep an actor on a set in which he can do little for the best part of a whole Act. But on the whole Miller handles and manipulates the cast skilfully as individuals and as of the Salem community, and the structuring of their movements is well organized and developed.

With this in mind, it is also worth considering how Proctor is gradually isolated in the play, just as he is as a husband and a respected member of the community: the structure reflects this. At his first appearance he seems dominant and dominating; but he goes off alone in Act 1 not to return; in Act 2 he is isolated in his own house in his uncertain relationship with Elizabeth, and then quite alone when she is taken off by Cheever. In Act 3 he has to fight his own battle against authority, and his self-revelation (97/88) isolates him even further. The whole play narrows now towards a fierce concentration on Proctor and his destiny, on his personal struggle with a greater evil than that pursued by the witch-hunters. Whatever is irrelevant to this burning issue of personal honour, integrity, principle becomes superficial and irrelevant. In fact, Arthur Miller's dramatic instinct that there must be this concentration led him to introduce a scene and reject another. At the beginning of Act 3 Miller inserted Cheever's strong assertion of Proctor's forthrightness (from 'I – Your Excellency' – 82/72, to 'I judge nothing' – 83/73) to emphasize this directness, and to concentrate and focus upon Proctor's character. On the other hand a very powerful scene, at the end of Act 2 and just before the Trial scene, between Proctor and Abigail, was eventually omitted, not as irrelevant but as distracting: again, spoiling the growing sharpening of attention upon Proctor's character, and disturbing the whittling-down process of his isolation.

It has sometimes been thought by some critics that the opening of Act 4 could be dispensed with: but it does set an atmosphere, of graver things to come, and is very quickly cleared: it puts the condemners in the physical setting of their victims, and closes our view of the pathetic figures of Sarah Good and Tituba. The rest concentrates entirely on the principals of the cast. Thus, as a whole, and in the elements comprising that whole, the play is carefully structured for the intensity and power equivalent to its themes of a life and death struggle in the cause of honour, truth, and justice.

Style

Style is a vague term: it concerns the author's method of approach and presentation, and is inextricably bound up with structure and characterization. A few points may, however, be useful.

Miller's diction, the speech of his characters, has a sharpness and an edge easily and naturally accepted because it sounds so natural and appropriate. Miller has the gift of using simple everyday language with surprising intensity. Without set speeches or 'purple patches', without over-long, heavy sequences (as are often found with, say, G. B. Shaw), using the most subtle rhythms and stresses, and by quick rapid give-and-take of dialogue, the language – which in a play is everything – is exciting, effective and appropriate to its historical and social context, powerful and often moving. Some of the elements of this diction are particularly interesting.

Firstly, there is the use of homely, normal, firm, basically monosyllabic language, as one would expect from the mass of ordinary untutored pioneering folk: and it has the ring of the historical period and the Puritanical atmosphere without these being forced and made obviously archaic or old-fashioned: remember that this must seem to approximate to the speech of people of the late seventeenth century sufficiently well for us to feel it is accurate and natural. It is simple, often rustic, sometimes a little primitive, in word and tone, often ungrammatical, loose, highly idiomatic: in other words, the vernacular, the common speech of plain folk. Obviously early examples abound: 'It were sport', 'she were swaying', 'weirdish', 'reddish', 'Be you foolish?', and so on. There is a constant dropping of the final 'g': goin', searchin', nothin', speakin', whippin', dyin', readin', and the like; and such dialect usage as 'I have trouble enough without I come five mile' still common enough in provincial England. Common errors abound, such as: 'What sort of soup were in this kettle?' and the double negative 'I didn't see no Devil', 'he cannot discover no medicine'. Sometimes the language becomes primitively coarse: 'I'll show you a great deal of doin' on your arse' and 'A fart on Thomas Putnam'. Less common is an unusual inversion or normal word-order for emphasis: 'That my daughter and my niece I discovered dancing like heathen ...' which in structure is typical of many sentences in Anglo-Yiddish, the Middle-European German-Jewish dialect of Jewry common among the first-generation refugees who emigrated widely in the late nineteenth century, especially to America: Miller's own family were of Austrian Jewish descent.

Then, the 'period' flavour of the late seventeenth century is rendered by the constant but not obtrusive use of dialect words or phrases, too many to list but nevertheless worth noting; and much of the language has a hard stern Biblical ring, with all the economy, familiarity and honesty of the Authorized Version: 'Abominations are done in the forest', 'stiff-necked people', 'dark as a pit', 'vengeance is walking Salem', and so on. And in many of the longer speeches there is a tautness, a muscular quality of structure and a basic Biblical flavour, combined with symbolic overtones, which makes the simple words and phrases ring out with remarkable intensity. A careful re-reading of the following – only a few examples of many – will help to reveal Miller's sure grip on his emotional packing of meaning and mood into an otherwise quite simple and ordinary vocabulary: the prose lifts from the page, and has the imagery and force, the rhythms even, of poetry:

23/*12*	Reverend Parris . . . her life too.
29/*18*	I know how you clutched . . . looked up at my window?
63/*54*	Since we built the church . . . meetin' houses.
72/*63*	If *she* is innocent . . . vengeance.

73/*64–5*   Proctor, I cannot think . . . open up our eyes.
74–5/*66*   Make your peace . . . will blow.
97–8/*88–9* In the proper place . . . must see it now.

Most of Elizabeth and John's speeches in Act 4 are also of this compact poetic strength: in fact Miller has made no secret of the fact that much of *The Crucible* was originally written in poetic form, and later 'chopped up' in case its actors would consider it a verse drama (say, in the type of T. S. Eliot or Christopher Fry) and develop an attitude towards it that would destroy the vitality of the language and theme. But the vein of poetry clearly remains, intensifying and concentrating the dramatic whole.

Frequently too there is the gift of a single phrase or sentence which summarizes with amazing emphasis all the emotions of an episode: poignancy, bitterness, frustration – concentrated into one crystal-clear compression, lines which seem indeed to have been tempered and purified in a crucible of the passions. Consider some of these in their separate contexts:

29/*18*   I have a sense for heat, John
33/*23*   There are wheels . . . within fires
43/*32*   Why Rebecca . . . today
60/*51*   She cannot think it
72/*63*   . . . vengeance is walking Salem
74/*66*   My wife . . . die for me
87/*77*   This man is killing . . . land
97/*88*   I have known her, sir. I have known her.
105/*96*   God is dead!
119/*110* It were a cold house I kept!

Other, equally telling, examples abound.

Miller had an equally sure touch with bouts of intense dialogue, where there is a sharp give and take of word and thought: some good examples are such as the conversation between Abigail and Proctor (28–30/*17–19*), the rising tempers among Putman, Parris and Proctor (35–6/*24–6*), Hale's interrogation of Abigail and Tituba in Act 1; many dialogues in Act 2; Danforth Proctor and Cheever (81–2/*71–2*) and Danforth and Giles (8–7/*76–7*) in Act 3, and much of the court questions and John and Elizabeth's encounter, in Act 4.

It ought to be mentioned how explicit are most of Miller's stage directions: but they will be projected to the audience by the actor's equally careful observation of Miller's instructions: he is fond of 'wide-eyed', for example: but others are more significant: 'innocently' (2/*8*), 'both afraid of him and strangely titillated' (28/*17*) are strongly charged with characterization; Parris's 'now he's out with it' (35/*24*) gives precisely the mood. A few others must be given, and others are there to be found by the interested student – and each should be considered on its merits and within its context.

42/*32*	*with a tasty love of intellectual pursuit.*
52/*42*	*it is hard to say . . . she receives it.*
53/*43*	*holding back a full condemnation of her.*
60/*51*	*He knows it is true.*
64/*55*	*delicately.*
71/*62*	*Or better still.*
95/*86*	*alarmed, quietly.*
115/*105*	*uncertain how to plead, for he is not accustomed to it.*

These are important, sometimes crucial, leads into a character's thoughts and development, and are essential features for an honest presentation and production of Miller's total conception.

Totally bound up with both style and language is the concept of imagery, the use of dominant ideas which thread through the play, holding together its symbolism. The title of the play is our first lead. Technically, a crucible (from a Latin word meaning a melting-pot) is a vessel used as a container for molten metals in various smelting processes. The literal usage – and remember that Arthur Miller is using the distant Puritan era of his own native country as an allegory for any historical time of an individual's personal stress – would thus seem to be derived from a vessel containing a mixture, a hotch-potch, of good and bad materials which is heated to extreme temperatures, so that only the pure metal, tempered and refined to an otherwise impossible perfection, remains to be tapped off. Metaphorically and symbolically, it is the eventually burnt-out purged and purified essence of Proctor's soul which is redeemed from the surrounding alien dross and rubble: after a long slow intense fire his light, reflected finally in his wife's face upturned to the sun, shines clear and supreme and all-conquering.

Of course, the Bible abounds in references to light and fire: everyone knows, and certainly the Puritans would have known, such references as 'Let your light so shine before men'

(Matthew, v, 16) and 'Then shall the righteous shine forth as the sun' (Matthew, xiii, 43); or 'The fire shall try every man's work' (1 Corinthians, iii, 13) and 'The vengeance of eternal fire' (Jude, viii). The imagery may be obvious, but is no less poetic and striking. Again, the notion of Hell-fire is Biblical (so remarkably imagined by Milton in *Paradise Lost*, for example) and witches, like martyrs, were usually burned at the stake (like Joan of Arc, condemned by the English as a witch).

Yet beyond this predominantly Biblical and religious source, the notion of the crucible can surely be taken a step further, although it is a concept not to be found in any known available information on Arthur Miller: it may, consciously or unwittingly, deliberately or coincidentally, be part of his thinking. Israel Zangwill (1864–1926) was an English author, of poor Russian-Jewish parentage: he wrote many novels based on intensely Jewish themes, but also some non-Jewish material. One of the latter was a play called *The Melting Pot*, where, in Act 1, a character exclaims: 'America is God's Crucible, the great Melting-Pot where all the races of Europe are melting and reforming! . . . God is making the American.' It is difficult not to feel that this, consciously or not, is a further element in Arthur Miller's choice of title and in his thinking and theme. The New England pioneers, the Founding Fathers and their Puritan followers, were the European originals of this stern unbending Christianity, just as the Jews, in Old Testament times, were the pioneers of a new religion, a new way of thought and life, in alien lands, beyond the fire-gods and the sun-gods of paganism. Now especially in the USA to which countless Jews and other wretched minorities fled from European persecution (as did the Puritans) in modern times, this huge mass of emigrants formed and reformed, assimilated and adapted, finding a measure of religious, social, economic and political tolerance, and a restoration of human dignity, after years of anxious insecurity and physical oppression. Perhaps Miller feels that, however painful and distressing, however much accompanied by sheer horror (like the obscenity of the witch-hunt or the concentration camp gas-chamber), this crucible process must occur from time to time, so that principles can be further purified, personal integrity again be proved, good triumphing over evil and thereby exposing even more starkly the horrors of that evil, each generation or era reforming itself, from the fires of Hell, or the prison crematoria, or the martyr's stake, from tyranny and injustice, only to emerge the purer, the cleaner, the finer when the heat of the struggle has died down. This aspect of the imagery, whatever the source, seems inescapable: it is a terrible but necessary stage of American, of all human, progress towards a more humanitarian civilization.

Not that Miller, within the play and at a more concrete level, has neglected to emphasize the fires of hell and the throes of burning through his play. From Tituba waving her arms over a fire for her 'black magic' and Abigail's reference to Proctor's 'burning' sexual nature, there are constant references to fire: 'There are wheels within wheels ... and fires within fires' (33/*23*); 'hellfire and bloody damnation' (34/*23*); 'obedience or the church will burn like Hell is burning' (35/*24*) are all from Act 1: there are at least four equally powerful images of this type in Act 2; and in Act 3 for example, 'We burn a hot fire here; it melts down all concealment' (81/*72*) and 'A fire, a fire is burning ... we will burn together' (105/*96*): and in Act 4 'if tongs of fire were singeing you ...' (120/*111*). The imagery is dominant, emphatic and unmistakable.

The characters

A glance at our Analysis of Miller's prose commentary (see Notes, p. 26) will show that, with the exception of Elizabeth Proctor and prosecuting judges, all the major characters are fully interpreted for us with Miller's own insight and intentions. It must nevertheless again be remembered that this commentary is available only to a reading public, not a theatre audience: on the stage itself, and this *is* a play, not a novel, these characters must reveal themselves and be revealed by others. Characters are displayed by what they say, and how they say it; by what they do in specific circumstances; and by what, and how, others say about them, coloured and prejudiced perhaps by particular emotions and relationships. Thus are they built up, in the round, piece-meal: on the stage, as we see them act and re-act, we gain insights into 'what makes them tick', what makes them who and what they are, how they appear to themselves and others. It is worth concentrating on this aspect solely from the actors' script, yet realizing all the time how much Miller's background commentary deepens and explores one's viewpoint. In the character-sketches which follow, the emphasis has been drawn from the script, and not the prose commentary. It is considered important, therefore, for several readings, to acquaint oneself with this background detail as a framework on which the play, as a theatrical venture, rests.

But it is equally important, after this reading and appreciation, to re-read the remaining script, the actors' dialogue, separated from the prose detail, so as to grasp how these analysed elements of character are revealed as the story develops. Then the full impact of one character upon another becomes clear in their interaction.

Take, for example, keeping solely to the script, the opening scene at the rise of the curtain: one takes in the visual setting, the kneeling, weeping praying priest, the inert small girl on the bed. A quiet mystifying opening: but the first words are spoken by an intruder, a negress, obviously very worried and distressed: the reaction of the man is one of fierce anger, even revulsion, and rejection; and then, when she is pushed out, he shows exhaustion and fear – and the audience wants to know why. Abigail's entry is different: her calling him 'Uncle' establishes their relationship at once. She is polite, correct, at balance: and thus the story develops, each entry building up, at varying pace, but relentlessly, filling in the details of character and plot into a purposeful, coherent whole. Different sides of character are revealed when uncle and niece vigorously discuss the dancing in the forest (19/7): Abigail is defensive, apprehensive, yet stubborn: Parris is frightened, alternating between shows of force and self-pity: with the mention of Goody Proctor, however, (20/9) Abigail's moods and attitudes harden. The entry of the Putnams (21/9) once again changes, realigns the moods, and quickly alters the atmosphere to one of malice and fear.

The entry of Proctor is especially important (27/16). It has already been noted that his wife, Elizabeth, has been significantly named: then, even more tellingly, Goody Proctor is named as the intended victim of Abigail's meddling with the occult (26/15), which provokes a violent reaction from Abigail as a truth which is obvious and dangerous. And within a few lines of dire threats, in walks John Proctor, causing various and varying reactions among the girls.

This is but a brief example of Miller's cumulative build-up of characterization, which does not end until each major character has played out his or her part and meets an individual destiny. It is important, then, to note the care and precision with which the detail of each action, reaction, and counter-action, in word, mood, atmosphere, is laid down piece by piece, as it were, to build up and eventually reveal the whole character as it moves, according to its make-up, through the play.

The Reverend Samuel Parris

There is very little good to be said for him

Parris, the middle-aged Salem pastor, is unloved and surely unlovable, frightened and indecisive in temperament. A one-time merchant, and the sole slave-owner of the area, he has come late into the ministry, and ought never to have done so at all: he does not understand children and the restrictive influences of rigid Puritanism on growing adolescent minds and bodies, and he believes that adults can be held to God by threats of hell-fire and eternal damnation. At the outset his greatest concern is less for the health of his young child than that the 'abominations' done in the forest may backlash upon his status and presence in the community, with which he is deeply at variance. This makes him servile to such malicious elders as the Putnams, who are a force in the town and in local politics, averse to Parris's original election to office. He is easily out-witted in argument with the shrewd and shrewish Abigail: he is petty, as are most men trying to justify themselves in an office for which they are ill-suited, and quick to feel anger and bitter resentment over such matters as his salary, his contract, and his fire-wood allowance: he constantly falls back on the stock unanswerable threat of hellfire and damnation: the tolerance, goodness and charity of God and Christ are not, apparently, part of his message and habitual way of thought.

Worse, perhaps, is his vindictiveness and lack of compassion. He is prepared to begin the savage torture of Tituba, who puts in the Devil's mouth much truth (48/38); he accepts the possibility of Abigail's own revengeful view of Elizabeth Proctor: in the Court Scene of Act 3 he forejudges with acute prejudice witnesses such as Giles Corey and John Proctor and their testimony even before it is given, and while it is being presented in detail.

The situation is, in a sense, that if he can shift the 'abominations' on to the Devil and his Salem associates, and away from himself and his family, and wipe off a few old scores along the way, he will have accomplished much and reasserted what he thinks is his rightful status in the community. Any evidence that the girls had been lying is of course highly dangerous to his cause and situation: he is pathetically, almost cringingly, clutching at straws to support his case, even though lives and impeccable reputations are at stake.

It is not until the end of the play that some of the truth dawns, after he has been instrumental in condemnation and death on the girls' testimony. Once he has been robbed, and the girls Abigail and Mary Lewis have run away, the truth is really brought home to his blinkered conscience: he sees, at least in part, the enormity of his involvement in human suffering.

His own life too has been threatened: the hunt has gone too far, particularly as he is now one of the hunted; too many obviously good and pious people have been condemned, and he has blood on his hands. And yet, after all he has done, he has the servile callous effrontery to offer a drink to the tortured Proctor, whom he fervently hopes will sign a confession of involvement with the Devil – at least, perhaps, one respected life will not be on his conscience. Proctor does not give him even that consolation. His last words in the play are a heartful cry to Proctor to save himself, and Parris. It does not come. This mean man, who has alienated himself from his flock by his hell-fire and his greed, his elevated ideas of status and trappings of outward show (63/34), is the basis and centre of all the hysteria and eventual persecution. Because of him, scapegoats have to be found and punished. He has no true Christian conscience; there is no sense of salvation about him in his self-seeking and vainglory. By the end of the play he has displayed more evil in himself than he originally set out to condemn in others, and is more of a victim than a persecutor. The irony is just and grim.

Abigail Williams

With an endless capacity of dissembling

Abigail is, at the age of seventeen, in common with her young friends, frustrated and over-restricted in her motherless adolescence among the stern Puritan moralists of the small gossip-ridden Salem community. Unlike the others, however, she has considerable beauty – and knows it – and she has been orphaned in the direst cruellest circumstances (27/15); she has a dominant even violent personality, especially when roused and on the defensive; and, especially, she has known the love (or lust) of the forceful, direct, respected (and married) John Proctor. It is difficult to judge, nor is it necessary to surmise, who is the more to be blamed: the passionate girl or the erring husband; each possibly led the other towards the cardinal sin, proscribed in the Ten Commandments, of adultery. But two things are clear: firstly, that it was a single, not a repeated act: and secondly, that Abigail wishes to have John Proctor for herself, by any means. Indeed, her reaction to Betty's revelation that she (Abigail) has drunk a charm to kill Goody Proctor (26/15) is characteristic. She well knows that they must all expect a thorough whipping for their pranks: she knows too that John Proctor has seen through their silly dabbling with Tibuba's voodoo incantations and mumbo-jumbo: but she also knows that she is no child, but a responsive woman. She uses Tituba as a scapegoat when Hale gets perilously near the real truth of the matter, and when Tituba – illiterate, superstitious slave as she is – is overpowered by Hale's inquisition, Abigail quickly, shrewdly and skilfully assumes her deadly role. She rises 'staring as though inspired': there is a cruel ambiguity here. Inspired she is, but not through external sources. This will be her design, her escape route. As for her uncle Parris, this diversion will provide scapegoat-victims enough for their own shortcomings and follies to be forgotten; the Puritan atmosphere, the whole climate of opinion of the time and place, favours the ruse. It is she who first mentions 'the rumour of witchcraft' and at the crucial point (49/39) seizes the opportunity and advantage. Her speech 'I want the light of God ... with the Devil!' combines the Puritan fervour of true religion, and the common folklore traditional forbidden heresy of witchcraft.

Abigail plays her chosen role with hideous perfection. We are given no insights into the initial reaction of the girls to their new-found, hitherto unknown, importance and celebrity as the dreaded centre from which such perverse wickedness radiates. As one expects, Elizabeth Proctor is soon, revengefully, caught up in the condemnation. Elizabeth reads Abigail's character aright: 'She thinks to take my place, John': and she will kill to do it. It is interesting to note that the two women never confront one another directly in the play, a discreet and subtle touch, this; when Elizabeth is called in Act 3 to testify (99/90) everyone, and Abigail 'with indignant slowness', is made to turn around, lest a mere glance reveal Proctor's dilemma, in having publicly committed his wife to utter only the truth. In those poignant moments there is no direct confrontation: and when Elizabeth leaves, and even Hale is convinced of the good wife's sincerity, Abigail again turns to 'inspiration' from the spirit world: she involves Mary Warren, who then indicts her master with Devil-worship. She has no more part in the play except to escape: what else is left? To save her own skin, she has deliberately sacrificed her man, now subject to the death penalty, his case having been disproved solely by her lies. She makes off while the going is good and attention is diverted, while Salem is rotting physically and spiritually to its foundations, robbing her uncle of his final security, and doubtless, as 'Echoes Down the Corridor' suggests, comes to a loveless haunted end. There is indeed something perverted about Abigail Williams: only the most blinkered and bigoted could possibly have seen in her a 'holy maid' like Joan of Arc, and there is something pathetic in her assumption of holiness and sanctity, if it were not certain that she knew them to be false and hypocritical. Cruel, spiteful, self-seeking, rebellious, vindictive, she is eventually betrayed by the very atmosphere she has vigorously promoted out of sheer malice and revenge and she hurts everyone whom she touches. She could not have done worse had she truly trafficked with and sold herself to the very Devil himself.

The Reverend John Hale

... where I turned the eye of my great faith, blood flowed up

Hale, at nearly forty, is one of the most interesting characters of the play, and must not be dismissed simply as a mere typical witch-hunter: he is carefully drawn and undergoes a radical transformation in his outlook. Alone among the persecutors he sees through the monstrosity of perverted justice and the frightful dangers of bigotry and dogmatism, of law and punishment trying to enforce morality. He is the only witch-hunter who has charity, in the full Christian sense.

In the opening Act he has all the enthusiasm and assuredness of a specialist among the illiterate and uneducated: laden with books and a parade of knowledge, like 'a young doctor on his first call', he thinks he knows all the questions and their answers. He is kindly, but firm, convinced of the concrete existence of the Devil and his works: his interrogation is painstaking and precise, thorough even down to the kind of soup the girls were taking. All is grist to his intellectual mill: everything is a possible clue, however vague or even absurd. But he does believe in human equality in the sight of God, be it the negress Tituba, the children or women; his educated intelligence reveals itself in many of the pithiest expressions of the play (such as, for example: 'what victory would the Devil have to win a soul already bad? It is the best the Devil wants ...', 'Theology, sir, is a fortress; no crack in a fortress may be accounted small', '... until an hour before the Devil fell, God thought him beautiful in Heaven'). All these are of the stuff of powerful, even unanswerable arguments for his cause; for him the Puritan cause is not merely strong, it is the ultimate strength, the basic orthodoxy. He cannot easily admit that human nature is so complex and various that a man may be good, even a good Puritan Christian, and yet not fulfil all the severe demands of the Puritan code.

But by Act 3 he has seen the truth. His speech 'Excellency . . . before we —' (100/*91*) marks the turning-point of his opinions. Every word after this shows a change of heart, sincerely held, and in Act 4 he realizes as much as does Proctor that the Salem community and Salem justice are in fact, through bigotry and a 'holier-than-thou' attitude corrupt and infected. No man knows when the harlot's cry will end his life (114/*104*): Hale has become even more direct, sarcastic, and a haunted conscience-stricken man. His faith, once held so lovingly and purposefully, has been shattered and degraded. He begs Elizabeth to make her husband confess to a lie, so that his life should be spared; Hale has indeed been broken so much by man's obvious inhumanity to man, in the name of law and religion, that he feels a life is worth a lie, even a very big lie, however monstrous and vile a lie.

Hale realizes, himself always above taint of suspicion, and quite beyond any meanness, ruthlessness or pettiness and with no axe to grind, that the very best intentions can indeed pave the way to Hell. What was once an eager intellectual duty in the relief of man has turned to dust and bitterness and terrifying despair. Of all the persecutors he realizes most fully the disintegration of Salem as a community and as a God-fearing state; at last, too, he understands the springs and passions of human frailty outside – indeed never contained in – the weighty books he brought in and flicked through in the first flushes of his enthusiasm to do the right. He is not afraid nor ashamed to lose face and status, and to pray among the wretches he has helped to condemn for a salvation he himself no longer deserves.

Elizabeth Proctor

It were a cold house I kept!

John Proctor's wife is among the few characters Arthur Miller does not comment upon outside the script: unusually, even her age is not quoted. She appears, technically, late in the play, fourteenth out of a cast of twenty-one: but she has been mentioned within the first hundred lines. Before her quiet entry, coming down from singing lullabies to her three small sons, we have had Abigail's vicious view of her, and something of Elizabeth's view of Abigail: she has even declined to attend church because of the girl's presence there, knowing from her husband's confession of his illicit liaison. We know too that she is often ill, a sickly woman, in fact; and that Abigail wishes her dead so that she can supplant her. What kind of woman is she in reality; what interpretation must be accepted?

Act 2 begins to reveal her essential nature: a good and kindly mother, albeit an indifferent cook – after all those years! – but infinitely tender and apparently charitable. She so wants to have her husband as he was once: but the Abigail episode has, naturally enough, hurt her pride and her religious status and upbringing deeply. She wants, she tries earnestly to find it in her heart to forgive John for his sin against the marriage-bond: but there is a point beyond which she cannot bring herself. Stronger in a sense than John, she sees how vital it is that he testifies, even though it may well mean public knowledge of their private shame. Each probes the other's honesty: unlike her husband, however, her view is that of strict Puritanism in its finest sense: and consequently she lacks real Christian charity, forgiveness, a touch of shown compassion for her tortured husband.

She well knows she will be among the condemned: 'Oh, the noose, the noose is up!': she has long seen through Abigail's guile. The poppet episode confirms it directly. Arrested by an uncomfortable Cheever and Herrick she goes, making arrangements for the security of her children: now her life could be utterly dependent on her husband's faith with the marriage-bond and his integrity. But she has yet to undergo further major tests beyond her wretched imprisonment and her developing pregnancy. In Act 3 she cannot bring herself, bearing his fourth child, to name her husband as a lecher, although his life depends on her telling the utter whole truth, not that she has been allowed to understand this aspect of the court's distorted rules of justice. In Act 4, brought in chained, but released temporarily, she has to resist Hale's burning persuasion to induce Proctor to tell a lie and confess to devil-worship.

This poignant encounter is revealing. She refuses to judge her husband even now, realizing full well his real goodness and positive integrity. Movingly, tenderly, she expresses her own past inhibitions, her shortcomings, her suspicions: she has been inadequate, unresponsive, has not matched his goodness with hers: at last, now, she can be wholly loyal to her man. She will not judge him: this he must do for himself. She remains silent during Proctor's mental torture, delicately not intervening as he is torn to and fro between an evil which parades as good, and a goodness which will be condemned. Not even the entry of the crippled aged Rebecca forces her to speak. She says nothing until Proctor decides not to confess to an untruth. He is to die – she could save him at the last, but she will not any more deprive him of a demonstration of his goodness. She has frustrated and restrained him enough: her Puritanical obedience, duty and devotion have been clearly inadequate and hollow, her marriage a façade through her own limitations. At this end she has developed a depth of understanding and a maturity of charity enough to let him go, even unto death, but a proud and honourable death. This much she can and must do for him.

Giles Corey

No man has ever been blamed for so much

Giles, aged 83 (and thus alive as a small boy of seven in England when Shakespeare died in 1616), is an extraordinarily vivid character: still physically strong and mentally sharp, he says little but wastes no words when he does speak. He is round and severe with Parris when the pastor talks more of money than spiritual service: but he is equally quick to recognize Parris's firmness under argument. He has a pioneering will to work, not to stand about making speeches; but he is not a 'bookish' man and cannot understand the temperaments of those (like his third wife) who are forever reading: this uneducated intolerance is to have grisly consequences. Although he stays (in Act 1) as he says to ask Hale 'a few queer questions' of his own, he asks nothing but the crucial one of the significance of such reading of books, which leads eventually to his wife's being swept up in the hysterical witch-hunt: he has said little but more than enough.

Nothing he can assert at the trial in defence of his wife can undo this unwitting accusation: he realizes bitterly that he has condemned her on the flimsiest pretext out of his own mouth:

he also realizes, swiftly, that land-grabbers are intriguing and conspiring to make the ill wind blow to some good in their direction. Walcott (68/59) and Putnam (87/77) are 'on the make' – 'This man is killing his neighbours for their land!' But he will not involve the innocent in any accusation; and when Proctor falls, he falls with him. His fate is gruesome, yet borne with that touch of the brave and forthright we would have expected from this tough old pioneer. His lips remain sealed because of the current law of inheritance: to deny the charge would have exposed him to death by hanging and the outlawry of his heirs: by remaining silent under the protracted torture of having more and more heavy stones laid upon him he maintains his position in law, asserting and denying nothing, and his sons may inherit the lands that otherwise Putnam, or any similar property-grabber, would have cheaply acquired. At the edge of death, with a grim humour, he asks for 'More weight', never submitting, never confessing, eager now to die as quickly as possible. His land, his heirs, are more precious than any higher principles, about which he probably knows little and cares less. He dies as he has lived, fighting for his rights, for his family, for the perpetuation of his name. There is a bold rustic simplicity about him which makes him pathetically alien, old-fashioned, yet individual, in the changing Salem which has lost its pioneering honesty and close community spirit.

Deputy-Governor Danforth

I will not deal in lies, Mister!

Danforth is the civil deputy-governor: in the absence of the Governor himself he is the principal officer in overall charge of the pioneer state. In the Puritan community, therefore, he rules the theocracy in all aspects of law and order, civil and religious. He has far more numerous and longer speeches, and is thus given much more weight, than the purely legal Judge Hathorne, 'a bitter, remorseless Salem judge'. In the major court scene of Act 3, for example, Danforth has over three hundred lines against Hathorne's thirty-three.

Danforth is a fanatic. He overrules justice from his lofty position of high responsibility, and is convinced of the legality and justice of the cause of the true religion. He will not have the court system undermined: any contrary evidence (for he has prejudged the whole affair anyway) constitutes such undermining. He is hard, cruel, unrelenting; even contemptuous of these lesser Salem folk caught up in affairs beyond their comprehension: any opposing pleas he treats as contempt of court: and petitions he uses as charge-sheets to swell the ranks of those arrested under suspicion.

It is untrue, or at least, too simple to say that he glories in his power: it is rather that he cannot afford to admit that the truth lies elsewhere. Convinced of the genuineness of the presence of witchcraft, and empowered to deal with it by the accepted means of harsh imprisonment, torture and death, he inexorably pursues what he must believe to be right. Thus he is dogmatic, bigoted, prejudiced: he cannot show any other side. He is appalled at such accounts of Proctor ploughing on Sundays, or Abigail laughing in church. The crux of his one-sided unalterably inflexible view is the speech in Act 3 (90/*80*): 'Mr Hale, believe me ... Have I not?' He has made everything rest on his testing of the children, and he cannot, will not, comprehend, cannot for one moment be brought to believe, that the principal condemner, Abigail Williams, is anything but a bewitched child – certainly not a potential murderer. He considers her and the others still children: he is in fact swayed by Abigail, and her 'trance' is overpoweringly successful as 'proof'. When Elizabeth refuses to condemn her husband, and name his lechery, Danforth is utterly reinforced in his original convictions.

He remains hard to the end: his victims must feel 'the perfection of their punishment'. He would have allowed Proctor's confession because it would have been further proof of the Devil's conquest in Salem: failing the confession he takes his life. He cannot afford to 'flounder'. Any exception made, any softness, any pardons, will seem to cast doubts on the accuracy and justice of his previous condemnations: 'While I speak God's law, I will not crack its voice with whispering.' He sweeps out of the play as hard and as callous as ever: life, reputation, family bonds – all mean nothing to him where God's law and will – as he interprets them – are involved.

Some critics have asserted that Danforth is evil beyond the needs of the play: but Arthur Miller has emphatically retorted that he believes such pure evil can exist and has existed. Some men, quite normal men outwardly, can indeed be responsible for monstrous evil because they do not fully know, or care to understand exactly, what they are doing: 'Evil is not a mistake but a fact in itself'. The history of religious and political persecution surely gives weight to this view. Danforth must be seen beyond the play, allegorically and symbolically. He sums up the human struggle between the individual and external authority. Ordinary levels of decency and common sense, fair play and honesty have no place here: Danforth cannot possibly admit any swerving from what he sees as his high cause: he is utterly dedicated, inhumanly possessed (ironically) in the moral conviction of his burning missionary truth. Cruel, possibly sadistic, he must continue the judicial murder so that the rightness of his case, as he sees it, cannot be called in question, as any evidence to the contrary cannot be tolerated in, and would destroy, a theocratic community. His role poses a religious counterpart, in many ways, to the political and social atmosphere of Orwell's *1984* or Zamyatin's *We*: power linked to bigotry and prejudice, blinkered to any outside influence or stimulus – however good the ultimate end is considered to be – is dehumanizing and appallingly destructive. Nor need one turn to fiction for examples: within living memory apparently civilized and developed states have found the leaders and their followers to organise deliberately in pursuing racial, political, economic ends through the obliteration of all who cannot agree with their doctrines. Danforth is no fictional monster: he is a type, a known example, a model. His attitudes, unlike his victims, have not been entirely laid to earth.

John Proctor

A kind of fraud

It must be obvious that as John Proctor is the central character of *The Crucible* even the shortest outline of his essential characteristics would repeat much of the material of the play. A few particularly interesting features only, therefore, will be explored here.

Proctor, the farmer in his middle 30s, is the key 'peg' on which Miller suspends his tragic view of the human condition. Proctor is the good man, with a fatal flaw, in a fundamentally alien and hostile society: ironically, and bitterly, in a society allegedly based on the highest moral and ethical principles. It is through Proctor that this society is exposed: his isolation within it and his rising above it on matters of principle make the tragedy yield its strongest irony – the sinner is less sinful and less criminal than his religious and judicial superiors because he has integrity, is not bigoted, and has an inner high morality by which he lives and for which he is prepared to die. It is a fascinating study of Miller's favourite reluctant tragic-hero type, and the historical distance of the Salem community of 1692 gives it, oddly enough, an intenser impact, inviting even more direct comparison to the sick societies of our own era.

This question of integrity is paramount. Life to Proctor is good: but he will not sacrifice his integrity merely in order to live. It is his 'name' which counts: 'How may I live without my name? I have given you my soul; leave me my name!' (124/*115*) But there is more to this than a mere personal gesture. By confessing, by submitting, by telling the big lie which Hale desperately craves, he will have allowed others to die who were equally innocent as he: he will not judge these others to be guilty at the cost of his own freedom. Honour is more important even if it must be reached through the fires of the crucible and the hangman's noose. Proctor will not debase himself: he will not comply because of force. Guilty on another score and therefore vulnerable because of a moment of moral laxity, the greater charge of witchcraft laid against him is, to him, absurd and almost irrelevant. But this is the charge which the whole of his society, the entire civil and religious organization, is pressing on him. His own real guilt cannot be lessened by public confession: his wrong deserves punishment, and cannot be made right by confessing to another fault. His conscience, he insists, must remain his own.

This makes Proctor different from the typical Puritan: 'We are only what we always were, but naked now' (end of Act 2). He is less worried as to what God will think of him, what God will make of his dying, rather than break faith with others who have not confessed, as to what his sons will think of him. He cannot be a fraud; he will not smash his reputation on a lie and yield to the sham, trickery, the base land-grabbing, wiping off of old scores, all the squalid motives which have lain behind much of the 'judicial' inquiry. He feels a responsibility to the world, outside his wretched, sinful self, and he dies in honour of that wider responsibility.

One could explore other aspects of Proctor's character and personality, of course. He will not suffer fools gladly: he is sharp and brusque with Parris over the priest's neglect of proper pastoral care and his obvious materialism. He is direct over basic essentials: when others are speculating on witchcraft and such 'fringe' matters, he has 'a crop to sow and lumber to drag home' – a sense that present labour is required for future security. He is the only character with any trace of a sense of humour, the only one who actually laughs openly (36, 55/25, 46). He is deeply sensitive over his wife's natural suspicions, for she knows that with girls such as Abigail it is rarely a case of 'once bitten, twice shy' for either partner: but Proctor's own defence of himself is surely sufficiently shamefaced and guilt-stricken: Elizabeth's suspicions and lack of charity, so long pursued, must seem intolerable and unjust. After all, he has fully confessed to her. How psychologically sound it is that when pressed by Hale he cannot recall, or bear to say, that one of the Ten Commandments which proscribes adultery! How subtle and delicate is Elizabeth's prompting here.

In a way, Proctor is the only 'whole' man of the play: this marks him down as its victim. His manliness impresses and titillates the frustrated young girls, and betrays him to one of them in an act of lust which is recalled emphatically as an animal gesture. For this he must be accused: but it is a private guilt. Whether he can be excused for it or not is again a matter for one's own conscience. He is in this and other ways a symbol of the changing times, perhaps even within the Puritanical state. Clearly much else has changed around him: the young ones show their frustration and rebelliousness to the anger and incomprehension of their elders; and these elders – or some of them – are endlessly concerned now over titles and other legal property-owning rights. As Miller comments, borrowing from *Hamlet*: 'the time is out of joint', and he might have continued as John Proctor very well might have felt: 'O cursed spite/ That ever I was born to set it right.' Proctor is himself certainly his own man, a new man. He is more freethinking, less tied to ancient ritual (much of which to him, anyway, is fundamentally un-Christian). He has a more liberal outlook even towards witchcraft as it is commonly and superstitiously accepted, for he sees that 'God is dead' indeed and the Devil does walk Salem when such men as Danforth and Parris 'are pulling Heaven down and raising up a whore'. Like Shakespeare's King Lear and most other tragic heroes he is very much a man more sinned against than sinning.

It may finally be noted that it is to Proctor that much of the 'poetry' of the play is given. He has most of the finest, purest, most haunting lines, some of them of considerable lyrical quality. 'It's warm as blood beneath the clods', 'Lilacs have a purple smell. Lilac is the smell of nightfall . . .'; and note also the final speeches of Acts 2 and 3, and the whole encounter with Elizabeth, his wife, in Act 4.

Proctor is characterized in considerable depth. When he dies a light goes out: but the fires of the crucible die away. It is a highly dramatic, theatrical, and symbolic touch that, after the harrowing drumroll, the final light of the play, the new sun of the morning, pours in on the place where he once stood. The man who was engulfed and isolated has found by dying a freedom for himself and others, and has by this brought back a light of sanity and reason to a world gone mad.

The other characters are all interesting and individually presented, but call for little detailed comment. Tituba opens the movement of the play: a servile superstitious creature in an alien and mostly hostile society loyal to Abigail even though the latter does not hesitate to use her as a scapegoat: and Tituba is seen once again at the end (a scene often omitted in repertory productions – mainly because it will involve the further character, and thus actress, for Sarah Good); a drunken and wretched creature awaiting her final call to her tropical home. But Tituba and Sarah are two of the outcasts of Salem society: the inner circle of the Puritan community are more clearly represented by the clique of girls dominated by Abigail: Betty Parris, Susanna Walcott, Mercy Lewis, Mary Warren (and Ruth Putnam, who is mentioned but does not appear). Each is briefly and sharply characterized within the script or Miller's commentary: Betty clearly frightened to the point of nervous hysteria; Susanna 'a nervous hurried girl', who seems plain and simple enough; Mercy, the Putnams' servant, fittingly 'fat, sly and merciless', hence ironically named, no doubt so used to being beaten herself that she recommends the same corporal tonic for the prostrate Betty as she has herself given to the ailing Ruth Putnam. Mary Warren, as the Proctors' servant, has a longer and stronger part, 'subservient, naïve and lonely', although she gains in confidence and self-importance as the trial continues. They all realize that their power lies in their unity, and that a crossed Abigail is a dangerous creature. At any and every moment of possible exposure they reassert their 'inspiration' to deadly effect, especially at the end of Act 3, when Mary Warren almost gives way to her tenderer feelings: but the cunning Abigail turns her confusion to devastating advantage.

The Putnams are fully characterized as vindictive, superstitious, distorted and opportunist: but they live. Rebecca Nurse, respected by everyone for her goodness and saintliness, goes innocently but boldly, even proudly, to her death. As Hale, in a vivid phrase, says: 'If Rebecca Nurse be tainted, then nothing's left to stop the whole green world from burning'. How pathetically sad is her apology to Proctor when she stumbles out to the gallows and he catches her, saying that she is weak because she has not eaten, while Danforth's snarled word of 'corruption' still hangs in the air. Her life and fate (for remember that Miller was dealing with the story of real, once-living people) prompted the American poet John Greenleaf Whittier (1807–92), a Quaker, and militant anti-slavery writer, to compose this simple touching epitaph:

Rebecca Nurse: Yarmouth, England, 1621
      Salem, Masschusetts, 1692

O Christian martyr, who for Truth could die
  When all about thee owned the hideous lie,
The world redeemed from Superstition's sway
  Is breathing freer for thy sake today.

Her husband Francis (some interesting detail is given in the prose commentary) has no power against the fanatic vigour of Danforth. Judge Hathorne is equally dominated by the Deputy Governor, to whom he is officiously servile. He is used technically and dramatically with skill, especially at the beginning of Act 4. He is more a presence than a rounded character, summed up as 'a bitter remorseless Salem judge.' The remaining characters call for no special comment.

General questions plus questions on related topics for coursework/examinations on other books you may be studying

1 Why do you find the ending of the play effective? If you do not, why is this, and how could it have otherwise have ended more effectively?

Suggested notes for essay answer:

1 Assignments demanding analysis of a theme must be handled particularly carefully: they require thorough pre-planning and drafting in note form especially (as in a play like *The Crucible*) where the writer provides practical direction, historical and other viewpoints, with explanatory background commentary in the opening Act. The text is a complete actor's script, tightly condensed and detailed, and needs methodical and patient unscrambling for specific purposes.

2 This question also involves some, but of course incomplete, portrayal of character. It is essential, therefore, that your answer keeps strictly within the limits of what is demanded – the study of a relationship: the balance must be controlled.

3 For this you must extract and consider (a) what the individually named characters themselves say and do (to whom, and how, and why); (b) what others say and think about them, in the same pattern, and (c) what the writer directs us to include. Totally relevant quotations must be extracted, and then integrated into your essay where appropriate: but do *not* rewrite chunks of the text.

Suggested outlines
Act 1

Note Abigail's earliest comments on Goody Proctor, under the goading of Parris, then to Proctor's entry and his encounter with Abigail: this provides the disclosure of the 'sexual' theme. Note too the further references to Elizabeth, and who says what. What is revealed suggests Proctor's strengths and weaknesses.

Act 2

The everyday 'norm' of the fractured marital relationship: note

the general atmosphere of strong feelings beneath the
apparently quiet, domestic rituals; how Elizabeth's 'coldness'
prevails, and why 'a sense of their separation rises' – her
suspicions about Abigail, Proctor's resentment of her coldness
and Biblical sense of moral justice. Explore the changes of pace
and emphasis of their various views, how the moral distance
between them seems unbridgeable, how the Salem situation
begins to impose its ominous influence, and also exposes the
basis of love that persists between them.

Act 3

In this exciting and moving trial scene Proctor defends his wife,
and learns of her pregnancy which may 'save' her for a year.
Here he admits to his misalliance with Abigail, which Elizabeth
will not 'confess' knowing: this condemns him. We already know
the facts, however, and apart from the intensity of their
protestations, little is added to our knowledge of their
relationship.

Act 4

This Act, in which Elizabeth is on trial, explaining her attitude to
Abigail, and where Proctor confesses his act of 'lechery',
develops the emotional tensions of the wretched victims of the
witch-hunt. Elizabeth affirms her lack of 'honest love' and her
moral inability to judge her husband: here too Proctor judges
himself, and will not yield to what he considers ungodliness. In
this desperate situation (he has been physically tortured, she is
physically sick) each has to make a crucial, moral decision, but
note that also they are spiritually and maritally closer than they
have been hitherto. Note their significant last words and actions:
neither has destroyed the other's integrity or humanity.

2 Summarize the essential story of the play in about forty lines.

3 Why do you think this play is called *The Crucible*?

4 Show how each Act builds up into a 'curtain-climax', and
describe carefully the factors which accumulate or accelerate in
the closing stages.

5 Which episode, dramatically, has (a) the most, and (b) the least
impact?

6 What details of *Echoes Down the Corridor* do you consider to be particularly interesting? Comment, with evidence from the play itself and not merely through speculation, on the inevitability of the destinies of Parris, Abigail and Elizabeth Proctor.

7 Why had John Proctor come to 'regard himself as a kind of fraud'?

8 Why does Proctor choose to die as he does? Had he, in the circumstances, any reasonable alternative?

9 Analyse carefully the relationship between John and Elizabeth Proctor throughout the play.

10 Why are Rebecca Nurse and Martha Corey condemned to death?

11 Do you consider Parris more than just one of the 'different aspects of witch-hunting' with Danforth and Hale? Wherein lies his greater importance in the play?

12 What part have the Putnams in the story? Is their role in any way significant: could they have been omitted?

13 Can one feel any sympathy for Abigail Williams?

14 Explain the importance of Hale throughout the play. Would the plot have taken a different turn had he not been called in by Parris?

15 What differences have you observed between the characters and personalities of Danforth and Hathorne?

16 It has been said of Arthur Miller's characters that they 'spring into life and far outrun their author's intentions'. Comment on this idea.

17 'It is very powerful drama, near to melodrama, but saved from that by its deep sincerity.' Where in this play have you found episodes 'near to melodrama'? Attempt to analyse the borderline between 'drama' and 'melodrama' from these selected examples.

18 'It is still a very effective play of action and suspense.' Illustrate this view by close reference to two or three episodes.

19 'If it falls short of the highest mark as a play of ideas, that is because Miller is attacking a cause – witch-hunting – that no one can conceivably defend.' Consider this carefully; what 'ideas' do you think are offered and pursued in this play?

20 Which parts (if any) of Arthur Miller's prose commentary have you found which spoil your enjoyment in reading through the play? Are there any scenes where you found the commentary particularly helpful in interpretation?

21 Arthur Miller has been praised for his 'muscular prose'. What do you understand by this? Locate and analyse some specific examples.

22 From your reading, show how at least two different writers (novelists or playwrights) have handled the theme of intolerance within a group.

23 Describe in some detail, from any novel or play you have studied or read, the actions and reactions to varying circumstances of a group of adolescent (teenage) girls or boys.

24 Show how an author has handled the theme of jealousy in any novel or play you have read.

25 Describe a character in a book or play you have read or studied who dies for a cause, and explain why he or she has no choice but to become a martyr to that cause.

26 Has any book you have read convinced you of the need for a country either to continue with or to abolish the practice of capital punishment? Give your own reasons for either.

27 Describe in some detail any piece of writing that has concentrated upon the influence of witchcraft or superstition on some individual, or within a group of people.

28 Show how any writer you have studied has handled the themes of the problems encountered (and how they were or were not successfully solved) by immigrants from one country to another.

29 Give a general account of any story you have studied which is set in a period of history before the twentieth century: include details of the differences between then and now.

30 Write a study from any book you know well which details the relationship between a husband and wife.

31 From your reading, describe the setting and atmosphere of any book or play in which belief in or opposition to a religious principle plays a significant role.

Brodie's Notes

D. H. Lawrence	**The Rainbow**
D. H. Lawrence	**Sons and Lovers**
D. H. Lawrence	**Women in Love**
Harper Lee	**To Kill a Mockingbird**
Laurie Lee	**Cider with Rosie**
Christopher Marlowe	**Dr Faustus**
Arthur Miller	**The Crucible**
Arthur Miller	**Death of a Salesman**
John Milton	**Paradise Lost, Books I and II**
Robert C. O'Brien	**Z for Zachariah**
Sean O'Casey	**Juno and the Paycock**
George Orwell	**Animal Farm**
George Orwell	**1984**
J. B. Priestley	**An Inspector Calls**
J. D. Salinger	**The Catcher in the Rye**
William Shakespeare	**Antony and Cleopatra**
William Shakespeare	**As You Like It**
William Shakespeare	**Hamlet**
William Shakespeare	**Henry IV Part I**
William Shakespeare	**Henry IV Part II**
William Shakespeare	**Julius Caesar**
William Shakespeare	**King Lear**
William Shakespeare	**Macbeth**
William Shakespeare	**Measure for Measure**
William Shakespeare	**The Merchant of Venice**
William Shakespeare	**A Midsummer Night's Dream**
William Shakespeare	**Much Ado about Nothing**
William Shakespeare	**Othello**
William Shakespeare	**Richard II**
William Shakespeare	**Richard III**
William Shakespeare	**Romeo and Juliet**
William Shakespeare	**The Tempest**
William Shakespeare	**Twelfth Night**
George Bernard Shaw	**Pygmalion**
Alan Sillitoe	**Selected Fiction**
John Steinbeck	**Of Mice and Men and The Pearl**
Jonathan Swift	**Gulliver's Travels**
Dylan Thomas	**Under Milk Wood**
Alice Walker	**The Color Purple**
W. B. Yeats	**Selected Poetry**

ENGLISH COURSEWORK BOOKS

Terri Apter	**Women and Society**
Kevin Dowling	**Drama and Poetry**
Philip Gooden	**Conflict**
Philip Gooden	**Science Fiction**
Margaret K. Gray	**Modern Drama**
Graham Handley	**Modern Poetry**
Graham Handley	**Prose**
Graham Handley	**Childhood and Adolescence**
R. J. Sims	**The Short Story**

ENGLISH COURSEWORK BOOKS